Just Tell Me What I Want

JUST TELL ME WHAT I WANT

*How to Find Your Purpose
When You Have No Idea What It Is*

By Sara Kravitz

NEW YORK

NASHVILLE • MELBOURNE • VANCOUVER

Just Tell Me What I Want

How to Find Your Purpose When You Have No Idea What It Is

Published in New York, New York, by Morgan James Publishing in partnership with Difference Press. Morgan James is a trademark of Morgan James, LLC.
www.MorganJamesPublishing.com

The Morgan James Speakers Group can bring authors to your live event. For more information or to book an event visit The Morgan James Speakers Group at www.TheMorganJamesSpeakersGroup.com.

ISBN 9781683504900 paperback
ISBN 9781683504917 eBook
Library of Congress Control Number: 2017903413

Initial Cover Design by:
Jennifer Stimson

Cover and Interior Design by:
Chris Treccani
www.3dogcreative.net

In an effort to support local communities, raise awareness and funds, Morgan James Publishing donates a percentage of all book sales for the life of each book to Habitat for Humanity Peninsula and Greater Williamsburg.

Get involved today! Visit
www.MorganJamesBuilds.com

Dedication

This book is dedicated to everyone who has ever felt scared to be who they are.

Table of Contents

Introduction

"Because maybe her secret self is actually her own personal prophet."

Glennon Doyle Melton,

Carry On, Warrior: Thoughts on Life Unarmed

When I graduated from high school, my senior quote was, "People always say you should be yourself, like yourself is this definite thing, like a toaster. Like you can know what it is even." This quote is from the epic 1994-1995 ABC television show *My So-Called Life*. If you're unfamiliar with it, you might want to watch before you read this book. If you've already seen it, you might want to watch it again because it's just that good. If you've seen it and have it memorized, then you should call me. Because we should probably be best friends.

"Be yourself" is like "follow your bliss," gems that fall under the category of advice that is "well-intentioned, but utterly infuriating." Originated by Joseph Campbell, "follow your bliss" was a phrase meant to inspire. It's meant to be an aspirational way to live. How bad could your life really be if you're "following your bliss"? Are you unclear about what path to take? Simply "follow your bliss" and know it's the right path. It's a beautiful idea. How, and why, would you argue with it?

However, it's since been co-opted by a lot of different industries in general and the self-help world in particular. If you're a millennial, you've probably heard "follow your bliss" several times over the course of your life, thanks to an ever-changing jobs landscape. The (good) intent being: if it's hard to figure out what you want, don't stress. Just "follow your bliss," do what you love, and the money will follow. The (less good) reality is often feeling increasingly frustrated because hearing that phrase over and over again does not seem to help in identifying what your "bliss" actually is.

This book is for anyone who's ever been told to "follow their bliss" and then immediately wanted to punch that person in the face. Same goes for "stay positive" or "be happy" or "stay grateful" or anything that is probably said with the best of intentions by the giver, but can come across as flat out patronizing if you happen to be the receiver. If you are someone who is even having a conversation with another person about "following" and "bliss," it is most likely because you are in a situation where there is a distinct lack of bliss, but you are completely unsure of how to change it.

The worst part is, you desperately want to change your life. You're not an idiot. You know you could change it, if you just had something to change it to. You know you are smart and competent, but are also haunted a little by the thought that if you were so smart and competent you would probably have this figured out by now. You know there is something out there that is not this, something that seems just out of reach.

So someone tells you, "Just do what you like." You immediately can't remember a single thing you like. They tell you, "If you do what interests you, you'll be good at it. And if you're good at it, you can make money from it." You rack your brain. You're pretty good at Instagram captions, eating whole boxes of popsicles, and buying books and then never reading them. Hmm, maybe there's something in that.

You want nothing more than to be successful. You want to be a #girlboss. You want to #hustlehard. You want to be someone you are proud of. Because you did things. Hard things and challenging things. You want to earn those feelings. You don't want to dread Mondays or work for the weekend. You can handle #nodaysoff if they are mostly #nobaddays. You understand gratitude journals. You want to be grateful for what you already have, but still dream bigger. You know you can work hard. In fact, you would love to work hard. You're so bored and frustrated that you're even ready to be deeply uncomfortable if it means getting you out of this place. Anything has to be better than this. You cannot have been put on this beautiful and terrible earth for this mediocrity. There simply has to be more.

You would love to follow your dreams, if only you knew where they were. Every time you try to identify even a single dream, they elude you. They seem to be the hidden treasure buried in the land of elves and ponies where your bliss also lives.

And, you begin to wonder, maybe you really don't have dreams. Maybe you were the one person born without any dreams or desires or even mild likes.

But what if you actually were born with... something. And what if you're just looking for it in the wrong place?

Tell me, what are your guilty pleasures? What are the things you're jealous of? What does your friend have that you would really, really like? What is the stuff that's hidden away that you're pretending doesn't exist? Let's sort through that stuff. Because that stuff is the key to what you want. It's in the darkest parts of ourselves, the parts we keep locked away. Because we are scared that's who we really are and someday someone will find out about us.

Much has been written about our "shadow" selves. The parts of us that make us scared or ashamed of who we are and what we want. The thoughts we keep under lock and key, and refuse to ever let see the light of day. The pieces of yourself you are confident will go away if you just ignore them for long enough.

The thing is, that *is* who you really are. And that's a beautiful thing. There's no part of yourself that comes from within you that can be wrong. It just can't. The moon is no better than the sun, the earthworm is no less than the butterfly, the vulture from the puppies. If it comes from you, do not be afraid of it. Question it. Ask it (yes, maybe even literally) why it's there. But do not run. It's there to teach you something. Just let it be there.

Also, you do not need to be an alcoholic or a cheater or something easier to pinpoint in order to have a shadow self. If you are just a "regular" person who lives a "regular" life, you too can have demons up the wazoo. And they are no less than the demons anyone else has to struggle with. They can cause just as much stress, anxiety, and paralysis. They are valid because they are yours.

This book will take you through the process of being brave. We'll take some of the things you're afraid of, deal with them head on, and then leap into the abyss. Because it's time. You might think that everything that is wrong with you needs to be eradicated; you might think that the only thing between you and what you want are those pesky little areas you are trying to make go away. You will not find that in this book. This book is here to tell you that all the things you are afraid to admit to yourself are the things that will show you the way. We all want what we want. I wish we could just accept that and get to going after those things. You deserve to have everything you want, no matter how ridiculous or unlikely it may seem. Because you cannot be brave without being scared first.

First, we'll spend some time getting to the heart of the issue. You might be afraid to even let yourself know what you want, let alone admit what it is. It might be stupid or embarrassing or out of your reach. We'll make sure you admit to yourself (which can be the most terrifying thing) what you want. It doesn't even matter why. You don't have to explain yourself to me or to anyone over the course of this book (or ever).

Next, I'll show you your fear is nothing you can't handle. Uncomfortable? Sure. Awkward? Most definitely. But all things you will be great at. I swear.

Once you start to understand it, we'll start to identify tiny actions you can take to get the ball rolling. The great news is you will definitely get results; the other news is this will take some work. You will 100% not be able to do everything you are doing right now and expect new and miraculous results. Sorry, my friend. Life just doesn't work that way. That being said, this is nothing you cannot handle and I will be here every step of the way. I take clients through this process on the regular. You will be so proud of what you can accomplish, and all that is imminent.

To accomplish something, we have to identify something. Maybe it's a physical object, a trip, a relationship, a job, an amount of money – any of these things work great. But we have to pick something, at least to start with. You can repeat this process over and over again, forever! But we have to start somewhere, and with something. This might be harder or easier than you think, but let's pick one thing and stick with that thing for the sake of this book. You can always call me and we can do this process together with something else (or read the book again!).

One note that bears repeating: when you are selecting something to pursue, the more specific the better – no matter how ridiculous. Specificity is key. The catch? It has to be something you actually want, not something you think you should want. I used to think I should have a real job, so I would pretend that's what I wanted. Now, that ship has sailed and I've accepted that what I actually want is to write books and be a life coach. I probably won't have a "real" job ever again. Once I actually admitted what I wanted over what I thought I should want, everything moved a lot faster.

Now, there might be some bumps along the road, so I've included some tools to help you navigate the process. When certain thoughts and parts of the ego feel like they're being challenged, they can have a really fun way of lashing out at us. It feels great! No, that's not true at all, but it's a part of the process.

However, with these tools, you'll know these moments might feel big, but they're not everything. They're also not anything that will prevent you from getting what you want. With these tools, you'll learn to navigate scary or negative things that may come up. There's no need to be afraid of any one particular thought or reaction over another. They all have something to offer. Everyone can have a seat at the table.

Once you've got your thing that you want and the tools to combat all the obstacles that are going to try and get in the way of you getting that thing, you can take action! Big, small, any step toward what you want is the perfect step. I prefer lots and lots of tiny steps (followed by lots and lots of treats), but there is no wrong way to do this. The only way to mess this up is not starting.

The last step is to jump. Take the risk. Do the scary thing. Make the embarrassing admission. Pursue the frivolous thing with reckless abandon. Jump, AND THEN TELL US ALL ABOUT IT!!! Seriously. Email me. I want to hear about it. All I want is to be around brave people all day long. Let me live vicariously through you and bask in your celebration. Bravery is contagious. Spread it everywhere.

So like we were saying in the beginning, "People are always saying you should be yourself, like yourself is this definite thing, like a toaster. Like you know what it is even." That quote actually continues on to say, "But every so often I'll have, like, a moment, where just being myself in my life right where I am is, like, enough."

Let's get you a million of those moments.

Chapter 1

Failure/I Hate Everything

This book is for people like you who think something is wrong with them because they can't think of a single thing they want to do. Or maybe you *can* think of something, but it seems too insignificant or embarrassing to pursue, so it couldn't possibly be your bliss. Because the only thing standing between you and a pain-free, super-happy life is this thing you keep hearing about called "bliss." Maybe some of us just don't have a bliss. What happens then? Welcome to endless unknowable life of sadness? Cool. Thanks. Now if you have a super-fancy life that you don't love that much, but love that it's super fancy, great! If you have a life/job/something that's working for you and you might have an inkling there's something more but you're cool for now, this book might not be for you. You can certainly stick around. You might learn something, but you also might want to take a beat and keep enjoying what you've got going on. Come back and read it when you're bored with your super-fancy life or are interested in what's next.

Why I Think Something Called the Dark Side Will Help You Get Happier

What is the dark side? How did I come to know about the dark side? What have I learned from spending time in the dark side? Why do I think it's a good place for you?

The dark side is the place where our socialized being is judging who we really are and want to be. What does that mean? It's the place within ourselves where we all feel like we need to be something other than what we are. It's the place where maybe how we were raised, or the values we've been taught to live by, are in conflict with our actual desires. It's where you feel like you shouldn't want what you want or you can't be who you are. Where you ignore the things you are, you've done, you want – so much so that you might not even remember they exist.

Because we assume our dark side is bad, it's easy to believe it's something that needs to be fixed or eliminated, or that it's somehow separate from who we are. But it's as much a part of us as everything we'd rather show off. The dark side is where we store the things we've done that we're not very proud of. We hide them there, and we don't tell anyone about this shame-filled storage place, but we don't make plans for sorting it out, ever. We think hiding these things is enough – out of sight, out of mind. We assume these are the things that are wrong with us, and we should bury them.

The dark side is where we punish ourselves for being who we are – for wanting what we want, for doing what we've done, for the parts of life we wish were different, or didn't turn out the way we assumed or hoped or thought they would. Maybe we think we have something to atone for, or that we have no right to forget. So we visit our darkness periodically. We keep ourselves in this place by reminding ourselves (somewhat frequently) of our failures and inadequacies. How can we ask for more when we've already squandered so much? We're still apologizing for the things we didn't get right. What gives us the right to ask for more?

The dark side is the place that, even after we've cleaned and organized and decluttered and bought flowers, we still feel off or strange or terrible about – the place we know we have to look, but rarely ever do. So we get another manicure, drink another green juice, double down on self-care. All lovely things. All very important. But ultimately just Band-Aids if we know we are avoiding something larger.

Imagine you left a bunch of family photos in the cardboard box in the basement. You should have put them in the plastic box your mom specifically bought for this. You planned to do it. You really meant to put them in the box, but you didn't. So when the basement flooded, they were ruined. Now you hold onto moldy, barely identifiable photos out of guilt – they are the family photos after all. Even though they've become decrepit, useless, and unrecognizable, they're still the family photos. Because it's hard to be the one to throw away the family records, no matter how gross they've become. Just shadows of their former selves – basically useless.

So now what? Hold onto rotting garbage?

This is your dark side. The things you are holding onto, the things you think are wrong with you, but are actually the rightest thing about you – even when they don't feel right yet. This is where the things that are right with you are born. It's where the seeds are planted, even if no plants have grown yet. Think of them as the compost before the worms get their hands on it. Those tiny little worms who, thanks to some earthly magic, can turn garbage into beautiful, healthy soil. Without that soil, you wouldn't be able to even think of growing anything. Sure it might seem like garbage now, but don't you dare get rid of it. We're about to bring in the worms. We are about to turn your garbage into the most beautiful, fertile gold. (Maybe I could have thought of a less gross metaphor, but at least now you can be assured this is not your typical self-help book. Or something.)

> *"Suffering can't be avoided," James Broughton told Jack Foley. "The way to happiness is to go into the darkness of yourself. That's the place the seed is nourished, takes its roots and grows up, and becomes ultimately the plant and the flower. You can only go upward by first going downward."*
> James Broughton, as told to interviewer Jack
> Foley, All: A James Broughton Reader

Broughton's thoughts might be a little prettier than my worm speech, but it's all cut from the same cloth. Maybe you cheated on your husband. Maybe you got fired after a week. Maybe you stole $10,000 worth of jewelry from a department store. How long will you punish yourself? Maybe you went to law school and on graduation day realized you didn't want to be a lawyer. Maybe you crashed your car into your neighbor's garage when you were drunk. Maybe it wasn't amazing that those things happened, but they did. So, now what?

Of course it might be tempting or logical to let these things affect every other thing you're going to do from now on. You might feel like you need to punish yourself, or deserve to be punished but, in my opinion, that's just stupid. And boring. You did something wrong. Do the grown-up, difficult thing and get over it. Forgive yourself. Let yourself off the hook. Because the alternative is garbage (kind of literally). If you spill milk, are you going to deprive yourself of milk forever? Really? Why?

The Dark Side Is All the Stuff You Think You Need to Change, But Don't

> *"I will boast all the more gladly of my weaknesses."*
> 2 Corinthians 12:9

Once you have seen all the light your dark side can bring, it is very hard to go back to believing the darkness is a bad thing. Sure, it might still be garbage, but that doesn't mean it's not also tremendously helpful once it's turned into something else. These parts of you might not be the shiniest, most evolved parts of you, but they are still parts of you. They're here. So let's use them.

You may stumble. You may forget the true meaning of the dark side. You may see a pile of pain and garbage and wonder how anything good could ever come from there. But your relapse will be temporary. You will mostly live in the light, but when you return to the dark you will remember this is a beautiful place too. It will feel different, and you probably won't need to spend too much time here, but you will return. And you will know that it is always in your best interest to leverage your dark side in order to learn things you didn't know and become a person you didn't think you could be.

Know, also, that the dark side is nothing to be afraid of. Maybe it's even the source of all your powers. There's always something to learn. Maybe you need to learn how you *don't* want to feel, or how you no longer want to live. Garbage is garbage. But garbage plus worms equals a chance for a new beginning.

The Disclaimer

I'm going to steer clear of things like murder, rape, and child abuse for this book. Not because I think those things are forgivable or unforgivable, but because I want to focus on smaller crimes of the heart and soul that can also cause massive amounts of suffering and guilt. And I don't think it's helpful to get caught up in the more challenging conflicts that can be used as distractions and allow people to continue living in their pain. Yes, those are valuable conversations to have, but this book will not be the place for it.

A wise person named Angela Lauria, who also happens to be my publisher, once said, "*Narrow the problem to what you can solve; don't broaden it so it becomes unmanageable.*" That's what we're going to do here. Punishing yourself is the easy option.

You're probably already really good at it. Forgiving yourself and moving on is hard. But it's also much more interesting.

After reading this book, I want you to feel like it's okay to want what you want. I want you to feel like your wants and desires are okay, no matter how self-oriented they might seem. Like you're allowed to be who you are. Yes, we all want world peace. But some of us also want to drink Starbucks every day without the guilt of reading a million articles about how if we just saved that money, it would become half a million dollars by the time we're 65. Sometimes you just want what you want. And sometimes what you want is a latte.

You Should Have This Figured Out by Now

"The main problem with this great obsession for saving time is very simple: you can't save time. You can only spend it. But you can spend it wisely or foolishly."
Benjamin Hoff, *The Tao Of Pooh*

God bless the mindfulness movement. There are so many mindfulness practices that, fortunately, have become more mainstream. Yoga, meditation, pranayama – we desperately need them all. We are busy. We are stressed. We have over-packed schedules and elevated blood pressure.

However, we also think we need to do a lot of things we actually don't need to be doing. This where the distinction between busy and productive is key. There is a ton being written about the myth and culture of business these days. Just Google either of those terms, and you will be inundated with brilliant (and not so brilliant) essays about the distinction between the two.

Here's the thing: I genuinely believe that people want to do the work. You probably have the sense that something is not working, but you also have the sense that you want to deal with it. You want to feel productive, active. Like an agent of your own life. You want to feel like they've made something – a thing, a difference, a meal. We were not just made to consume, but to create as well. But when people don't know what they want, action turns into meaningless hamster wheels of busyness. The idea that if you simply do enough things, satisfaction will appear. The hope that one day, quantity will eclipse quality.

A to-do list can become synonymous with a list of achievements. At the end, I will have achieved something. Then I will feel accomplished. My self, the self that is me, will be validated – finally, a reason I am on this earth. The sense of accomplishment, and the subsequent praise that might come along with that accomplishment, can be a drug. As long as someone tells you you're doing a great job, you don't necessarily have to think about whether or not you're doing a great job at something that actually fulfills you. As long as someone thinks you're good, you don't really have to think about whether or not you care about being good at that thing.

What? That's crazy.

That's like saying, one day I will berate myself enough so that it suddenly turns into being nice to myself. Or, I can punish myself enough for the decisions I've made, and all that punishment will one day make me okay with them. It's like Louise Hay says in *You Can Heal Your Life*, "Remember, you have been criticizing yourself for years and it hasn't worked. Try approving of yourself and see what happens." You can't critique your way into loving yourself. If you are not satisfied with what you're doing, someone else's enthusiasm will never take the place of your own satisfaction. You have to love all of you, right now, no matter what. That's the deal.

So, no. You shouldn't have it figured out by now. Why? Because you don't. And neither do a lot of other people. But you're here, you're asking questions, and you know something should be different, so you're on the right track. Also, what if you figure everything out perfectly, and then it changes? Does that mean you did everything wrong? Or does it just mean you're a living, breathing being that's constantly evolving? Of course your needs and wants are going to change over time. And, thank goodness for that.

What If I Don't Have a Bliss?

It's possible you don't. I might not even have a bliss. Bliss to me sounds like lots of sleep and coffee. I take that back. Not only do I have a bliss, I have two of them.

The thing about "bliss" is that it's tainted by images of joy, zero effort, ease, money, etc. But the truth is that bliss is not effortless. Maybe your bliss is the thing you think you're really terrible at, fail at most of the time, won't make you any money, is embarrassing to say out loud, but for some reason are still willing to do anyway. So the idea of bliss becomes less about ease, and more about doing more of it no matter how awkward or strange. Bliss equals engagement. What are you willing to engage with over and over again? What are you willing to be wrong about and still want to learn more? What are you willing to be legitimately terrible at, and still want to give it one more try? What if bliss wasn't synonymous with ease, but with interest?

Maybe you have a thing you clearly want to do, but the hardest part will be declaring yourself – declaring to the world that this is the thing you want to do, and then giving the world a chance to have an opinion about it. That's a scary thing to think about. Maybe you have tons of supportive people and no idea what you want. Which means you only have one more person so win over: yourself. That might seem even scarier. Maybe the idea of admitting things to yourself is even scarier than having to admit them to other people. What if following your bliss meant admitting your most embarrassing desires? Or just any desire? What if it meant that you are actually a vulnerable human who has to admit you want something and run the risk you might not get it? And everyone will know you didn't get it. But mostly, *you* will know you didn't get it.

Newsflash: that's exactly what it means. I am from NYC, wanted to be a writer, and became a life coach. People move to NYC because it is the land of possibility, the place where anything is possible. The flip side of living in NYC where anything is possible, is living in NYC where anything is possible. To be constantly surrounded by people who are making something out of nothing is inspiring – until it is suffocating. You see all these people with focus, drive, and clarity. They seem to work hard without impediment. And they all have brilliant ideas. How much did the world really need my ideas when they could have those people's ideas? Plus, their ideas are shinier. The people who had them dressed better. It made me feel paralyzed.

What this meant was that I had a super-fun, judgmental wall to break through before any of these things could actually happen. It meant I had to declare to the world that I was a life coach and still take myself seriously (which, when condensed into one tiny sentence does not sound that hard, but trust me – it was very hard). How could I want something this ridiculous? And I wasn't even totally sure, it was just the only thing I could think of at the time. I just had to actually take seriously the things I thought were my cheesiest, stupidest, most frivolous desires. And then share them with the world. No big deal. This is why we might want to consider never allowing bliss and ease to be in the same sentence.

If Everyone Followed Their Bliss, Wouldn't the World Grind to a Halt?

Shout out to *My So-Called Life* again (because you can never make too many MSCL references). "It's such a lie that you should do what's in your heart. If we all did what was in our hearts, the world would grind to a halt." OMG, that show is everything. It kills me. Even now, 20-plus years later, I know almost every word and want to watch it every day.

Here's the thing: the people who wrote those words were following their hearts. I don't really know anyone who goes into the "safe" world of television writing. It's definitely not on the list of fallback jobs to take if you're someone who breaks out in hives over not knowing where your next paycheck is coming from. I'd also rather test drive the idea of everyone doing what was in their hearts than not. Remind me what the downside is of too many happy people?

That said, the pressure to "do what you love" and "find your bliss," as we've talked about, can be suffocating. For people who can't answer the questions, "What would you do if you knew you couldn't fail?" or, "What would you do if money wasn't an issue?", not having an answer can make them even more paralyzed.

Maybe a better question is, "What do I hate the least?" or "What are my guilty pleasures?" or "Who am I jealous of?" I want people to explore the things they might be scared or ashamed of if something blissful is the most readily available option. People's dark sides are rife with possibility and I think we gloss over them too quickly to get to the shiny, happy, assumed stuff. There's so much in our darkness and it's nothing to be ashamed of. What if everything you wanted was just on the other side of everything you are scared of?

The Idea of Pain vs. Actual Pain: Why "Follow Your Bliss" Is a Lie

I know "joy" is thrown around a lot in the life coaching community. Words like "joy" and "delicious" and "bliss" are used in excess and can sometimes create an adverse effect (or at least they did for me). How could I imagine joy when all I wanted was "not actively terrible"? All I had to do was follow my bliss! Silly me, of course. Why hadn't I thought of that? Was I the one person without bliss? What did it mean that nothing gave me joy? *Maybe I'll never have any bliss, so I guess I'll just be living in a cardboard box if anyone needs me.*

Just Tell Me What My Passion Is and I'll Do That

There's so much encouragement for us to "be positive!" and "stay positive!" Do we think that if we shout "choose happiness" loud enough, it will drown out any sadness or uncertainty? That if we bully our anxiousness enough it will magically reconfigure itself into sheer joy? Of course it would be really great if you could just wish these things and they would come. Maybe some people can do that, and more power to them. I wish only lovely and good things for everyone. Of course, I want people to be happy and positive. I'm just not sure that aggressively telling someone to "be happy" is the way to achieve it.

What if we don't feel light? What if we don't feel positive? What if it's all built on ashes instead of bedrock? The dark side clearly exists. We've all experienced it. So why are we pretending it's something that can/should be vanquished?

Why are we so afraid of it?

A few years ago, I was at a conference hosted by author and life coach trainer, Martha Beck. At the event, Martha mentioned something about how humans are the only creatures who commit suicide based on their perceptions of a future so enormously painful that the easier option becomes not being alive. Now I'm not sure if I got my notes right and I don't have the scientific studies to back this up, but it struck a chord with me. I believe we are scared of the idea of pain more than the actual pain itself.

Aren't you in pain now? Being struck, frustrated, overwhelmed, aimless – that's its own special place of hell. Yes, making changes might be awkward. You might stumble a few times or try something that doesn't work or have to do something twice, but how could it possibly be worse than where you are now? Could trying something new really be that much worse or harder than staying in a life that doesn't look or feel like you?

As someone who spent a lot of time feeling stressed, guilty, and ashamed for feeling that way, I get it. Being raised in NYC and graduating college without any student debt – those two things alone made me feel like I already had so much handed to me. And I just couldn't make anything work. I had an education, a fresh start, and the privilege of youth. I had everything I needed to be "successful" and still couldn't get it together. The shame of that grew and grew. I took jobs that were handed to me. I worked really hard until I hated them. And then I would quit, or be let go, wondering why I couldn't even keep the easy, nothing jobs I hadn't even tried to get.

It's impossible to talk about the dark side without talking about avoidance, shame (hey Brené Brown!), depression, and isolation. However, the counterpoint to all these things is the resilience and strength and beauty that is everywhere, especially where you least expect to find it.

I understand if you want to roll your eyes here. I would too.

Would You Rather Be Happy? Or Would You Rather Be Right?

The darkness is the thing that would rather be right than be happy. Have you ever had that kind of fight with someone? Where you were right, and said all the right things, and the outcome was exactly what you wanted and still, somehow, you felt terrible? This is the game the dark side plays with you. The dark side wants to prove that it's always right. It will eat any shimmer or glow or blink of light that you spark within yourself because the darkness does not want you to be happy – it only wants to be right. It wants to prove to you that everything is dark anyway. Don't bother changing because it's all dark anyway. You want to try and get a new job? All jobs suck. Are you trying to lose weight? Don't bother, you'll just gain it back. The darkness does not allow for the possibility of change because it would rather be able to say "I told you so," even if getting to do that means no one is happy. If you are putting yourself in a situation that conflicts with your core values, with who you fundamentally are as a person, no matter what you do, it will be hard to feel better about it.

How to Start Figuring Out What You Want: Put Yourself First and Very High Up

Others are putting themselves first. And that's what you should be doing. Fill your cup so much that it's not only runnething over but it's getting everywhere and is now a flood risk. Take out the noise of other people and reconnect with yourself. Get all the manicures. Take all the yoga classes. Plant all the flowers. Write all the words. Go to all the concerts. Sing all the songs. Do what you need to do to feel fulfilled. Give yourself everything you are looking for from other people. Give it to yourself so you're not disappointed when someone else doesn't give it to you. Give it to yourself because you really deserve it. Even if you've screwed everything up. Especially if you've screwed everything up. Because if we are lucky, life goes on. So celebrate it. You learned another lesson. Praise hands emoji.

Do Less

Or better yet, do nothing. Sit still. If every second of your day is filled with activity, good or bad, helpful or not, it's still full. If it's full, then nothing new can get in. Give something a chance to get in there. To arise. I wish I could give you a worksheet for this one. But there isn't one. The worksheet is really a tracker for how many times you actually allowed yourself to sit still and do nothing. Start with five minutes. Just sit there. Work your way up to 15 to 20. Remember this might be deeply awkward or uncomfortable. But so will most of the things asked of you in this book. It will be good practice.

I had an amazing, beautiful, hard-working client who wanted a new job. Or she thought she wanted a new job. She wanted a change and assumed her job was the thing that had to go. She was a very creative person and she was not in a creative job. It seemed like a no-brainer. However, once we got into it, it became clear she was deeply exhausted. She had two-year-old twins, had just moved, and had finally found good daycare for her babies. She wanted to write and she wanted to be creative, but she also wanted to sit still for a minute. After moving and the new responsibility of not one, but two, little people, was a third upending change really what she needed? Maybe eventually, but right now? No. This woman needed a break. She needed a minute to sit and exhale and let the dust settle. The last thing she needed was to kick up a whole bunch of new dust.

So that's what we did. We created ways to make her life easier, more peaceful, and more enjoyable. Plus, with a full-time job and little kids, she didn't need things to add to her to-do list. She needed things she could outright eliminate, or that required practically no effort and could fit into already existing tiny pockets of time. So we created a full-on ease rebellion. Every day, the first thing she did when she got to her desk was to write for 10 minutes (I am a huge advocate of Julia Cameron's *The Artist's Way* – another example of how if you jump ship for that book, I will totally understand). Then everyone else could have as much of her time as they needed. But at this job she didn't love, that already took up so much of her energy, those first 10 minutes were hers. Eventually we worked our way up to 10 minutes first thing in the morning, and 10 minutes at lunch, but we started small. Starting small (even smaller than you think) helps create the habit. After that, we made her desk a really warm and inviting place. Since she was spending so much time at her desk, it only made sense to make it a beautiful place where she wanted to be. Photos of family, a framed quote, flowers, whatever it took to make it a tiny sanctuary where she wanted to spend some time.

Then she mentioned she loved cooking with her kids. So once a week, she would pick a recipe, take them to the grocery store, and then they would all cook a recipe together. They had to eat. She had to go to the grocery store. Why not make it a fun event for everyone? And that's how we made her life better without her quitting her job. We took the things that already existed and elevated them, plus we carved out new time for herself that created zero stress. Sure, one day a new job might be something to look into. But since the quality of other aspects of her life were elevated, her job automatically needed to check fewer boxes for satisfaction, so she could stop, breathe, enjoy, and then make a decision from a place of calm, instead of panic and overwhelm.

Start Listening to Your Intuition

Okay, this one might be a little more challenging if it's new to you, but it's worth mentioning here so you get the most practice with it. Here's how to begin. Just get still. Sit still (and you're already good at this because you did it earlier). Be still. Even if you're not actually that still, imagine that you are. Once you're somewhat comfortable, start noticing what comes up.

Remember, there's no need to be an A+ student in listening for answers. Don't try that hard. Do a mediocre job of listening for answers. They rarely come loudly. They rarely hit you over the head. And why should they? You're already lucky enough to have them looking out for you. They shouldn't have to shout and beg for your attention. You should be accommodating to them. It's also very probable you will hear something and say, "That's it?" or "I already knew that." That's totally normal. Maybe you know something, but aren't doing anything. So you'll hear that message until you do something different. It's never a bad idea to say "please" and "thank you" before and after. Also, sometimes it's just not that deep. Sometimes all my body asks for is a deep breath and an iced latte. Sometimes it really is that simple.

The Dark Side Is a Liar That Keeps You Honest

"Take chances, make mistakes. That's how you grow. Pain nourishes your courage. You have to fail in order to practice being brave."
Mary Tyler Moore

Remember, as we talked about earlier, the dark side is the place where our socialized being is judging who we really are and want to be – the place we know we have to investigate in order to start reconciling our wants, facing our fears, and moving forward. The darkness can be scary because it might seem like there is nothing in it that's familiar. It might be full of things you think need to be different in order for you to have a shot at getting the things you want. But it can also be freeing because nothing is familiar. It's uncomfortable so you feel every moment. You can't glide past anything because you've done it before so you know how it'll turn out. That level of hyper-awareness is how things finally get through – you're less numb and more awake.

The dark side can be a catch all. For anything and everything that has ever scared you. Because we might think of it as this vast empty hole, it gets to be whatever it wants. Because we don't name it and give it a defined identity, it gets to be as big and scary as it wants to be. And if it comes from our egos, it's probably going to want to feel pretty powerful and important.

So, let's name it right now. What are the things you need to change? Both the things you want to change and the things you feel you should change? What are the things you want, but think should be different? The darkness is the layer of judgment you put on what you want, so you've already trapped yourself before you've even started. That's why it feels so terrible and confusing. You can go in circles, endlessly torturing yourself for being who you are.

We can't give the dark side that kind of power. We can't give anything that much power. That power is for ourselves. If we can name a fear, identify the judgments, get really clear and specific about what it is we're scared of, it becomes a defined entity. When we give it a name and a face and a personality, it gets smaller, it becomes more manageable. We can get to know it more intimately because known entities are less scary than unknown ones. The fear is no longer an amorphous blob that can shapeshift away from us, constantly hiding and making us scared because we don't really understand it and therefore don't know exactly what to be scared of.

The fear itself doesn't want to be vanquished, so it will just expand itself to include whatever new, imagined, bigger fear you've come up with. This means it never has to even do any work! It just gets the benefit of being scary without proving why. How is that even remotely fair?

If it wants to be worthy of being something to be afraid of, it should have to apply. It should have to state an objective, write a cover letter explaining why it's the perfect fear for you, and gives at least three letters of reference for why it should be considered to be a new and worthy fear for you. Applying to things is a pain in the ass. It's time consuming, it rarely works, and it makes you have to think about whether or not this is something you want to put effort into. Start thinking of your fear in the same way. Would you really hire someone who doesn't have a job description, rolls in to work whenever they want to, and who you're unclear about how much money you're paying to, but it seems to be a higher number with each passing week? You would never hire that person. And yet they are working for you right now.

I had an amazing client who was convinced he had an untapped wealth of secret talents he had never accessed. He dreamed of the old Soviet Union tests where they would evaluate you when you were a child, guesstimate what you were good at, and that would become your job for life. He assumed he had gotten as far as he did (which was pretty far – financially, reputably, and socially), but his real talents were deep down, hidden in a place where only the Soviets could find them. He was skeptical that his 30-year career he had mostly loved was enough of an indication that the vast majority of his talents had not only been unearthed, but used quite successfully.

His fear (the vast number of talents he would never know about) kept him at a job he desperately wanted to leave. Because his brain was doing a great job at keeping him safe. Out there in the land of untapped potential, there could be saber-tooth tigers who were very excited to eat him. Safely tucked away at his job, he could dream of any number of talents he had that were just hiding from him without any foreseeable way of ever knowing what they were. Hello, amorphous blob fear.

We looked at whether or not this claim was likely to be true, or whether his fear had found the perfect thing to say to him to keep him where he was. We looked at whether there had been a time when he hadn't felt like this. What was he doing at this time? What was different between then and now that made him aware of all these talents he supposedly had, but never occurred to him to use? (The answer was a job he didn't really love, a daughter going away to college, and a growing awareness of the passage of time and how he wanted to be spending his.)

So the answer was actually in his fear. His fear was asking him to question how he was spending his time. Because he wasn't spending it on things he wanted, so the fear actually turned his attention to the problem area. The difference was he believed that just its presence alone meant something must be wrong. He hadn't considered the possibility it could, in some way, be beneficial. Together, we could explore his fear and find out that it was actually directing him to the root of his stress. He actually did want to be spending his time in other ways.

So we created a plan to make sure he was spending it how he wanted to. We made a pie chart of all the things he does in a day, and how much time is spent on each. When he complied with his ideal breakdown, he was happy. When he didn't, he got stressed. Having a more visual way to see how he was allocating his time allowed him to feel like he had more control over how it would be spent.

So, Do It Afraid

> "The shadow is not only the place where we keep the nasty and monstrous underside of ourselves. It also harbors 'vitalizing instincts, sleeping abilities, and positive moral qualities,'" says Daryl Sharp in his Jung Lexicon. If developed, these unripe aspects might become talents and

treasures. Unfortunately, because they are intermingled with the parts of us we don't like to look at, they often remain untapped. In shunning our shadows, we shut ourselves off from some of our potential brilliance."

Rob Brezny, *Pronoia Is the Antidote for Paranoia, Revised and Expanded: How the Whole World Is Conspiring to Shower You with Blessings*

You're scared of getting fired. Having no money. Dying alone. Never accomplishing anything, let alone what you really want to. How do I put this? *Everyone feels this way.* Does that make it better or worse? Both? That's fair. On one hand, you're not alone. Everyone thinks they're going to die alone in a cardboard box at some point (or most of the time). But it's also so boring because your fear is just the same thought, on repeat. Like, the same thing, over and over and over again. Sometimes there's a variation, but mostly it's the same thought on repeat. How boring is that? You're better than that. I promise you. You really are. Risks need to be taken. This, my friend, is bravery. And courage. And exactly what you need to get anything done.

Something to Try: Name Your Fears

Write down the three things you're actively trying to avoid most. Maybe one is something about you you're embarrassed by or wish you could change. Maybe another is something you want, but are afraid to tell people about. Maybe a third is a situation or a circumstance you want to change or wish you could change. Anything you shy away from, hide from other people, don't want to admit to yourself, or wish you could change is fair game.

If you're having trouble thinking of them, try free-writing. Just total stream-of-conscious writing for 30 minutes or three pages. See what comes up for you then.

Also, don't worry if the list isn't perfect, or exactly right. We just need a starting point. Don't make "not thinking of things to put on the list" another point of shame.

For more exercises, recordings, and pretty worksheets, hop over to sarakravitz.com/toolkit and download the toolkit now!

Chapter 2

Your Fear Is Boring

"I Wish I Could, But I Don't Want To"
Phoebe Buffay, *Friends*

Last night I found an email I sent to an old boss. It was vicious. Not totally unmerited, but scathing. In it, I harshly criticize the way he handled a conflict, elaborate on how disappointed I am in him, and ask him to, moving forward, put all of our correspondence in writing. It's a bold email, especially from a 25-year-old who was kind of in the wrong. And while it's always nice to see that you are capable of sticking up for yourself, that's not the point. I never should have been at that job. I knew I needed to get out, but had no idea how to go about doing it. So I just blew it up. That email, that job, that situation only existed because someone told me to "give it a chance."

I knew it was wrong after a week. I stayed for 10 months. Because that's what you're supposed to do at jobs – stay at them. I slowly, and not so slowly, developed hate in my heart. I had a client yell at me each time I talked to him. My superior would tell me things to say to him, and they would just make him yell more. And, honestly, I didn't even know what we were talking about most of the time.

I was scared of looking crazy or irrational. Like I couldn't hold down a job, or didn't know what I was doing. I wanted people to take me seriously and I thought having a job, paying rent, and acting like other functional members of society was how to do that. I "gave it a chance" because I didn't know what to do other than quit. And quitting was shameful. My instincts were in direct conflict with society's tenets, and I didn't know at the time that you should always chose yourself over society.

So I stayed. I started openly mailing it in. My business casual turned into plaid shirts and skinny jeans. I wrote darker and darker emails, passive aggressively baiting my superiors. I stopped doing part of my job because it made no sense and because I just didn't want to.

I didn't know it at the time, but even though I thought I was stuck, my essential self, the truest part of me, the part uninhibited by what society or my parents thought, was working hard to get me out of that situation. I believed I was trapped forever. The part of me that was concerned with appearances wondered how I could possibly expect anything to change. I wasn't applying to jobs, I wasn't networking, and I was continuing to show up to work and do the bare minimum necessary to receive a paycheck. In my mind, there was no way out. I wanted the sky to open and an answer to fall out of it. I wasn't doing anything to change my situation, but I wanted a big, obvious, iron-clad answer that would tell me exactly what I needed to do to be happy.

What I didn't know back then is that when we are in situations we're not meant to be in, forces start acting on our behalf to get us out. We are looking for grand actions and what we may be getting are subtle hints. I couldn't tell you what any of the subtle hints were that I wasn't picking up on back then (it's possible the rage and crying were decent signs). I only started picking up on them when they were consistently obvious, but I didn't know what to do about them. When we are taught we should be lucky to have a job and need to stay there a minimum amount of time in order to satisfy some invisible requirement that doesn't make us look like damaged goods, it can be hard to see anything past getting through the day.

So the email was my way out. Looking back, I had to have known what would happen once I sent that email, and that's probably why I sent it. I didn't know how to get myself out of the situation, so I let something else figure it out for me. It wasn't the prettiest way out, but it was certainly effective.

The whole email thing coincided with a meeting I was due to have with the Executive Vice President about the work I was no longer doing. And it happened because right before that meeting, my direct supervisor handled a relevant situation in a totally sketchy way, so I sent that scathing email to him and the EVP criticizing how they handled it. A totally fair move on my part but, as I found out, totally frowned upon. Apparently corporate white males who are technically your superiors and already insecure in their power roles don't always like it when you make suggestions on how they can be better at their jobs.

So we sat down at the meeting, which I'm sure some people could have gracefully handled. I am not one of those people. It already wasn't panning out to be a comfortable meeting, and 30 minutes before it started, I had gone and set a fire. I listened to the EVP list all the things I'd supposedly done wrong, as well as a few that he *actually made up,* and then was supposed to sign a paper that I'd heard his complaints and agreed with them. He asked me if I agreed, and I heard a voice come from somewhere and say, *"Get out now."* I quit on the spot. I knew that if I didn't, I would be abandoning a part of myself that would take a long time (if ever) to recover. They were actually surprised. I guess they were just used to people being angry and hating their jobs. They thought it was normal. I did not.

In an increasingly changing world (especially the job world), it is easy to cling to that which promises answers. It's totally understandable to be tempted by the road that offers safety and security, emotional and financial stability. Here it is! All laid out so nicely in however many steps! Everything you need to do to prevent dying alone in a cardboard box! But if it's a road you don't want to go down, how safe can it be? No matter how many chances you give it, will you ever find security in a world that looks and feels nothing like you? Where your instincts don't match your surroundings? Maybe at first, maybe for a while. But eventually, later on, maybe 10 months in, you might feel differently. Like something is wrong and what was once a safe choice is actually now a threat to your sanity. Just remember, when people tell you to "give it a chance," they're really telling themselves to give it a chance. They're using you to justify staying with all the things they want to quit but can't. Or think will magically start working the longer they continue to do it the exact same way. End rant.

So, go ahead, "give it a chance." Or don't. But, like, really don't.

Resiliency Is Your Spirit Animal

> *"If it scares you, it might be a good thing to try."*
> Seth Godin

The dark side and the stories that are written from it are actually the antidote to any shame you might feel about your particular dark side. They are the chance to reclaim an unfortunate event and wear it proudly like a badge of honor. It's harder to be ashamed of something if you've just heard a beautiful, well-crafted story about how it was something the other person used to get them where they are today. It might not be something they are happy to have happened, or would ever wish on someone else, but these are our lives. The mission then becomes about how we can use ALL aspects of our lives to create the best circumstances.

I worked with an amazing client named Kelly, who came to me for career coaching. She was very young, but had already been working in the restaurant business for over 20 years. A restructuring at her company gave her the opportunity to think about work, its place in her life, and what she would like to be doing. In our conversation, she mentioned her love of interior design. She had majored in it in college. She was the friend and family member called upon whenever a room had to be re-designed or a paint color chosen. Her voice got lighter and quicker when we were talking about interiors. I asked her why she hadn't pursued it professionally. She told me about how her father had worked in restaurants, she'd been working in them her whole life, and how it honestly never occurred to her. Her family worked in restaurants, so she would work in restaurants. It was literally not a thought in her head that you could choose your job based on an interest or what you enjoyed. It never occurred to her you could find your job fun. This was definitely something we needed to challenge in our work together.

She told me she was probably too old to go back to school and start over. She had probably missed her chance. Yes, of course, now it was perfectly clear to her she should have gone into interior design, but oh well. These things happen. That door was apparently locked and dead-bolted.

She had also recently gotten her broker's license, and was planning to start selling real estate. So her goal had basically become to get as close to the houses as possible, but never allow herself to do what she really wanted to do with them. How mean is that? So we went to work processing her shame around making the wrong choice and forgiving herself for anything she didn't know 20 years ago, but knew now. She was all set to commit to a life of punishing herself for making the "wrong" choice at 22. She assumed she had made her bed and now the only thing left to do was lie in it. Talk about dark.

Now she's actually taking the classes she needs to be an interior designer. It's not even remotely going to take as long as she thought it was going to, and she's working with the home stagers at her real estate firm in the interim to help get her feet wet. Had she not investigated the things she thought she should punish herself for, she never would have used her "biggest mistake" to understand she had the right to make a new decision for herself. Not to mention that 20 years of managing restaurants made her a whiz at budgets, working with contractors, interacting with clients, and managing staff. Basically, it was all intensive job training for the role she had always wanted to have.

You may hear a story like Kelly's and think, "Well, at least she knew what she wanted to do." That's true, she did. But she was also prepared to live the rest of her life never actually doing that thing. Kelly's story shows that we all are working with what we are given. It wasn't too late for her, and it isn't for you.

Feel the Fear and Do It Anyway

One of the most brilliant things anyone has ever said. This might actually be one of the top five, all-time Rules for Living. Fear and action can co-exist simultaneously; one does not eclipse the other. In fact, the two together create the conditions under which bravery is born.

One thing I do know is that after I take a risk or say something new/freeing/scary about myself, I feel good. Better. Freer. More in touch with myself. Proud of myself. And that's the point. The point of doing all these scary, new things is to know myself better, so I can be proud of who I am and what I do.

Stop Making Things Work

A very brilliant friend of mine once said, "Just because you can make it work doesn't mean you have to." A lot of us come from cultures where quitting is one of the worst offenses one could commit. We are surrounded by messages that we should dig deeper and hustle harder. If something isn't working, it's simply because we're not working hard enough.

Guess what guys? Not everything works. Sure, you could probably make it work. But at what cost? Why? Is it because you actually want the thing to work? Or is it so you won't think you failed at making it work? Or that you quit?

Why is quitting so hard for us to do? Is it really so bad? Think of all the people who quit smoking. Or quit drinking. Or quit a life of crime. Sure, those are pretty easy examples of how quitting is actually the noble thing to do, but why isn't quitting a job you hate, or even moderately dislike for the promise of something better, considered noble? I think taking a chance on yourself is pretty noble, and if that means quitting things you're comfortable with, but don't especially love, more power to you.

When I think about my last job, the one I quit, I am sure I could have made it work. I could have buckled down and worked harder. I could have learned more and produced more. But I hated them and they were terrible people. So how was giving them more of my time and energy ever going to work out for me? Was the goal to one day be promoted high enough that I wouldn't have to talk to any of them? No. I hated the work and I hated them. The idea of further entrenching myself in that environment was absurd. So quitting became the smartest option.

Quitting says nothing about you. Quit your job. Quit your marriage. Quit the thing that really should be working by now and just isn't. Of course you could make them work. You're a smart, capable person who could make a lot of things work. But do you really need to? Stop doing terrible people favors. They don't deserve it. Why give them more of your time and talents for them to squander? Maybe it's something we all have to go through in order to learn it's something we never have to do. But, let me be clear, you really don't have to.

What Are You Tolerating?

Another very smart lady who was one of my teachers in Life Coach Training sent out a newsletter a little over a year ago about tolerations. I still have it flagged in my inbox. It was such a powerful message about the things we can make work, the things we can put up with, but have questionable reasons for doing so. Why tolerate things when we do not have to tolerate things? Her story is about a page-a-day desk calendar she realizes she doesn't like. She never remembers to tear off a page every day, so when she does she knows exactly how long it's been since she last did – just a minor taunt that she's been living in error. Plus, this calendar was something she won in a raffle, so it felt harder to throw away because it was a prize! Prizes are supposed to be fun, and how often do we win things anyway?

Of course, after throwing away a bunch of back pages, the quote she landed on was, "The space for what you want in your life is already being filled with what you are willing to settle for." ~ Carolyn Strauss. Of course. Add up all the tiny little things that annoy you but you deal with because they aren't that big of a deal, and you get a much larger cost. Imagine what it might be like to live your life if you let go of somethings that you weren't that attached to anyway.

You Could Always Sell Cat Toys

One of my most driven clients was stuck in a mess of tolerations. This was a woman who had a full-time job that afforded her a lot of benefits. She wasn't interested in leaving, but was sure her job was already on the road to being eliminated. She wanted to start a side gig that she could build over time, and that maybe, if necessary, would one day become her new career. It didn't hurt that she was super bored at work and wanted do something that actually required the use of her brain. My client was so open to any option, she had started an online business selling cat toys. She figured that since she loved cats, this would be a logical next step.

The reality, however, was very different than what she had pictured. Her time was spent monitoring inventory, commissioning blog posts, and making sure shipping was on time. All tasks she was mostly fine doing, but weren't really any more interesting than what she was doing at work, and they weren't generating the level of income she had hoped. However, she was hesitant to stop because she didn't want to be the miner who quit digging six inches from the unearthing the biggest diamond of their career.

So she continued to send monthly emails about cat toy inventory and proofread blog posts that were sent to her. She was slightly more than breaking even. It was enough to justify continuing, but she didn't really want to. It wasn't bad, it wasn't good – it was all fine. Again, she was afraid she was within whispering distance of success and would be the person who quit right before all the money started pouring in. A totally legit concern. But, if the money started pouring in and now her job was to orchestrate cat toys for the next five years, would she be happy doing that? She started her side gig because she was bored. Was this going to be just as boring? Was she going to be okay missing the cat jackpot if it meant getting to do things that challenged her more?

We talked about what she really enjoyed, and I learned she loved to plan, research, and orchestrate systems. She loved to learn about new things, create systems for those things, and then implement them. Every time one of her systems was a success, it made the other parts of her job worthwhile.

I asked her whether, if she could make the same amount of money as she was making with the cat supply business, but in a job she liked more, she would switch. She said, of course. So, we started exploring transitioning her cat toy business into something she might enjoy more. We set her up with a new side business that was more in line with the things she actually enjoyed, not just tolerated. She became a virtual assistant for a small, woman-owned business, reviewing the components of the business that needed help, and then putting systems in place to keep everything organized, and eventually grow the business. Within, like, a day, she was already making what she made with the cat business. After a week, she was making significantly more and, gasp, was really enjoying herself. Who could have guessed that? All by reducing her tolerations.

Not Everything Has to Have a Moral or a Takeaway

Sometimes we are afraid and then we are not. Sometimes we are afraid and then we work really hard to move through it. Sometimes it sucks to relive things and recreate things. Sometimes it's amazing. Sometimes you just have to do it. Sometimes it works, and sometimes it doesn't. But there's no way of knowing which until you try.

They're All Gonna Laugh at You

Does anyone remember that old Adam Sandler skit/joke/ song, "They're All Gonna Laugh at You"? No? Good, you shouldn't. From what my inner 12 year-old remembers, it's basically just him repeating over and over again, "They're All Gonna Laugh at You." And maybe they will. But Adam Sandler makes millions of dollars making movies with his best friends. So let's just all laugh together on our way to the bank.

Something to Try: Calibrate Your Body Compass

Here's another tool to help you get to the bottom of what you want. The good news is that if you've ever played the children's game Warmer/Colder, you have some experience with how this next tool is going to work. Also, if you've been trying to think your way out of this problem, this one might be a little bit of an adjustment. I'm certain that quite a few of you are hyper-cerebral, highly intelligent, analytical people who are incredibly good at dissecting problems or situations in order to uncover the most rational, logical, and helpful solution. There is no doubt in my mind you are quite good at this. If it's your job, I'm sure you're amazing at it. Your pro/con lists are without a doubt better than most. Here's the thing: that part of your brain will not be helpful here. For this tool, we're going to use the rest of your body that comes with your brain. You might have heard about a mind-body connection, or have read an article or two about how scientists are finding that there are a lot of neurons in your gut that mirror your brain. If this sounds a little touchy-feely, just go with it for now. Remember, for this to work you have to test things out of your comfort zone. You have to do things other than what you're doing right now. This is how things change.

Here's what we're going to do: for the next few pages, we're going to momentarily suspend any disbelief you have and act as if we can get answers about our next steps based on what our body is telling us. This is a technique taken from Martha Beck (that you can read more about in her spectacular book *Finding Your Own North Star*). She calls it the Body Compass because it uses physical sensations in the body to determine things we want more of and less of. Often these physical sensations are obscured because we spend much of our lives suppressing our natural desires in order to mimic the socially acceptable desires as dictated by society, rendering us very polite, well-meaning, clean-cut members of a social environment that might be killing us. If you feel devoid of the ability to know what you want or how to figure it out, this might be a result of years of impeccable social grooming. Your success at fitting yourself into the molds society has nicely created for us has made it much harder to identify the wants of your individual self.

First, let's calibrate your Body Compass. You'll want to put yourself in a pretty relaxed position, where there's as little stress and tension in the body as possible. Lying down is totally okay. If you're in a chair, make sure you're actually comfortable, and not just assuming you're comfortable. We'll use a scale from -10 to +10. I assume you know how a scale from -10 to +10 works, but just in case, a negative 10 is like the worst feeling ever; positive 10 is the best feeling ever.

First, think of a bad experience you had. *Please do not think of the worst thing that ever happened to you.* Pick something that was bad, but not catatonic bad. Maybe a -6 to a -8. Now put yourself back in the memory of that experience. Close your eyes and put yourself back in the place you were in, the clothes you were in, the street you were on. Remember the people that were there. Replay the events that happened.

Now notice what's going on in your body. Not just your words and verbal responses to what's happening, but the physical sensations that are showing up. Is there tightness, heaviness, rock-like sensations, pain? Where in the body are these things occurring? Are they moving? Are there smells, colors, anything else occurring? Now name this sensation. Is this the "Tight Chest" feeling? The "Pit in Stomach" feeling? Maybe "The Black Cloud" feeling is more apt? Name it whatever will make you know exactly what this feeling is the second you hear it. It's about to become the way you'll identify situations you should move away from.

Now let's calibrate the other side of the scale. Think of a relatively pleasant time. Doesn't have to be the absolute best time of your life, but a time where you thought, "This is something I wouldn't mind happening again." Put yourself back in that scenario. Surround yourself with the clothes, the people, the environment. Notice the physical sensations arising now. What are they? Take stock of their texture, caliber, severity, place in the body. Stay in it another minute. Now what is the name of this sensation? Again, make sure you call it something you'll recognize as this specific sensation. Maybe this is your "Honeymoon" feeling? Or your "Edge of Your Seat" feeling? Any name that makes sense to you is perfect.

Congratulations! You now have a functioning Body Compass. Now you can play an advanced version of Warmer/Colder. If you're doing something that shows up as a negative on your Body Compass, do less of that. If it's registering more on the positive side, do more of that. Is this more Black Cloud feeling or more Edge of your Seat feeling? These feelings don't need to show up as 100% in either direction, but they will probably lean toward one at least slightly more than the other.

Here's where it gets confusing.

Let me give you a personal example: Writing a book shows up at about a +8 on my body compass. When I think about it, I literally get a chill. However, each and every step I have to take in order to get a published book *does not show up as a +8 on my Body Compass.* Writing books is my bliss. Writing a book is not a totally blissful process. There are moments of bliss. And when it's really hard, I know that it's work that makes me feel proud of myself, and that makes me feel better. But every second that I am writing is not blissful. Not even close.

And this is why it's stupid to tell someone to follow their bliss. Because most bliss is not easy. Writing makes me feel like I'm getting somewhere, like I'm figuring out a problem or making progress. *But it doesn't make me feel blissful.* Actually it mostly makes me feel agitated, like there's just a *ton* of energy in my body and sometimes it's hard to sit still (which can be a problem when 90% of writing a book is based on sitting still for extended periods of time). But agitation does not necessarily mean annoyed, it's just a lot energy that I've placed a judgment on. It could just be all the words that are really excited to jump out of the airplane that is my body. Who knows? The point is that following your bliss can be a lot of awkward and uncomfortable work. But it's also work that makes you proud of yourself for doing it. And you can use your Body Compass to help figure out what that is.

Chapter 3

None of It Is Wasted Energy

"For what it's worth: it's never too late or, in my case, too early to be whoever you want to be. There's no time limit, stop whenever you want. You can change or stay the same, there are no rules to this thing. We can make the best or the worst of it. I hope you make the best of it. And I hope you see things that startle you. I hope you feel things you never felt before. I hope you meet people with a different point of view. I hope you live a life you're proud of. If you find that you're not, I hope you have the courage to start all over again."

Eric Roth, *The Curious Case of Benjamin Button*

For all the late bloomers out there, I hear you. This is for you. As my brilliant medium (the kind that talks to dead people) uncle once said to me, "None of it is wasted energy." Man, how I didn't really believe him at the time. It seemed like such a convenient thing to say to a minimally employed 20-something-year-old. Something you say to a kid immersed in the anxiety of a family who doesn't understand why they won't just get into law or healthcare. A kid who seems to go out of their way to avoid any type of gainful employment or give their parents any type of break in easing their stress over whether this kid might one day be able to take care of themselves. (Shout out to everyone who is raising their hand right now!)

And even now, as I write this book, more on a path of anything I've ever wanted to do in my whole life, it still seems too easy. "None of it is wasted energy" – it's something you say to people who are floundering. It's a kind lifeline you throw so they don't go home and eat a pint of ice cream. I can just imagine him slightly tapping into my thoughts because they were something I never could have shared, getting a hint of the conversations that were happening in there, and then gently closing the door behind him. Then casually lobbing that out to me as I walked by him in the living room. Never saying anything more, or anything less. Maybe even knowing it wouldn't land for years, but during that time, it would serve as something almost aspirational for me. Maybe one day I would truly believe that none of it was wasted energy, and until then I would just continue to hope that things would somehow, magically, work themselves out.

Consider this your whispering uncle (well, aunt) moment. None of it is wasted energy. Trust.

What If There Is No Good, Easy Stuff?

What if you have just struggled up until this point? Does that mean it's just over for you? That's your hand? Always and forever? It can't be. It actually has to mean you will be the strongest person ever when you decide to see how all of these things are just part of the path to get you where you need to go. Of course, these obstacles are not nothing, but do they have to be everything? Can they be how you acquired your wisdom, strength, and resilience? They are the assurance that you haven't come this far to only come this far.

"*We tell ourselves stories in order to live*" is one of Joan Didion's most famous quotes. Are the stories you're telling yourself helping you live? Are they helping you grow, or are they keeping you small? Are they even your stories? Meaning, were you told certain things are how they are and always will be that way? Or can we find a way to create new stories in order to help yourself live better? Is it true that negative events in your life can only have negative effects, or is there another possibility?

Do the stories serve you? Stories can be actual events you've lived through or witnessed, but they can also be invisible tenets, an arbitrary set of rules we've structured our lives around. Some of them we've been living by so long, we don't even see the possibility of challenging them, like Kelly and working in the family business. It never even occurred to her to question it. And that's fine, they're usually not meant to harm us, but now would probably be a great time to start investigating yours. What are the things you've always assumed to be true? (A common one: "I have to work hard to make money.") Or, what would happen if you changed them? Do you think you're allowed to change them? If it's all just the past, a mass of things that have already happened, and there's nothing we can do to change them, why can't we either let them go or make them work for us? Maybe even get ahead of them. My hope is that some of the stories I'm about to share will inspire you to re-think, repurpose, and re-imagine some things in your own life.

> *"The past doesn't exist except as a memory, a mental story, and though past events aren't changeable, your stories about them are. You can act now to transform the way you tell the story of your past, ultimately making it a stalwart protector of your future."*
> Martha Beck, *How to Stop Regretting Decisions*

There is no "true" version of a story. There is no "real" version that you have to honor or live by or punish yourself for. They're all just memories. Some carry more weight than others. Even if you are the one person on earth who carries the most perfect memory of an event and you know exactly how it went down, what everyone was thinking while it happened, how they were feeling, what their intentions were – now what? What are you going to do with that perfection? Is this the kind of crown you can wear? Or is it kind of useless? What if you just forgave yourself because it's over and is never coming back? Or what if you used your story as a gift for someone else?

My client Isabella is a beautiful, strong, and intelligent woman – self-made, ran her own business, had three amazing children. And had a truly terrible marriage. A husband who was selfish, self-loathing, didn't work, was around long enough to cause drama, and then took off the second he made things really bad. She knew all of these things, and yet she stayed married. "At least he picks up the kids from school sometimes," she would say. "And drops them off at hockey on the weekends."

Um, no judgment, I know people get married for all kinds of reasons, but I didn't realize that hockey drop-off was one of them. Isabella was living with the story, "I can't get divorced. I can't have another failure in my life." She wasn't allowing for the possibility that staying on her road to success, staying in her marriage, *was* the failure. Not letting herself off the hook was the failure. Not realizing that just because things didn't turn out the way she thought they would or the way society would have preferred didn't make the time she and her husband spent together or their children a mistake or a failure.

Sometimes we put so much pressure on the *outcome* of a situation to know whether it was a success or a failure, it doesn't allow us to get anything out of the experience itself. If the only way to tell if a marriage was successful is when it's over (because one of you is dead), is it safe to argue there maybe could have been better alternatives? All to say, the past is what you make it. You do not have to live captive to it. Make it work for you. And if there is something you know for sure can never be positive or used for good, absolve yourself. Shave a sliver off its power over you. Nothing should get to have that much power over you. You are powerful beyond measure.

Question Your Shame

This is a tough one. Or at least it was/is for me. As someone who spends a lot of time investigating thoughts and patterns of thinking, there are still some thoughts that trip me up. Here's one of my big ones: *I should have this figured out by now.* I'm XX years old. Why don't I know what I want? Why don't I know myself by now? Why does everyone else have this figured out and I don't? If I really was that smart, wouldn't I have a lot more money by now?

These are the thoughts that would visit me late at night. Or in broad daylight. Despite truly knowing and believing that thoughts are just these things that float around in our heads all day long, these are the thoughts that can seem truer than all the other thoughts. Sometimes I know better; sometimes they know better.

Here's the real question: ARE THEY TRUE?

There's an incredibly brilliant woman named Byron Katie who one day realized that basically none of our thoughts are true. The only things we have are reality and the present moment. Or, as Eckhart Tolle put it, "The situation is always neutral." The situation at hand is what it is – nothing more, nothing less. The thoughts we have about those situations and the judgments we put on them are what cause distress. Buddhists call this "suffering."

So taking the thought, "I should have this figured out by now" as an example, we ask, "is that true?" Is that true in the same way that we need oxygen to breathe, and there is salt in the ocean? "I should have a bliss." Really? Should you? Why do you think that? Is that really true?

The great news is that Byron Katie has these great worksheets called, "Judge Your Neighbor." Take a thought that's been creating a lot of stress for you and, as Byron Katie would say, take it to inquiry. Start to see why it's been giving you such a hard time. Maybe start to loosen the grasp it has on your life. Maybe it's true, maybe it's not. But maybe other things are true as well. Is it an either/or scenario? Or are other things possible? Let's find out.

Second Guess Your Thoughts

One thing to try is take something that causes you pain, that you absolutely assume to be true, and begin to poke holes in it. Do you know for sure this thing is true? Or have you just spent a long time assuming it was true? Is it possible that it's not? Sometimes we are holding onto thoughts that are painful simply because they are familiar. Yes, we know they're not helpful and we know we need to desensitize ourselves to them in some way, but deep down we also know it's easier to hold on to them. Yes, it's pain, but it's also familiar pain. We already know how it will hurt and we already have appropriate coping mechanisms. In our brains, familiar pain seems better than unknown pain.

To practice, take a thought you feel is true and that also causes you a measure of pain. Something like "I don't know what I want," or "I will never find a job that I love," or something different, but equally painful. Notice the physical sensations that arise in your body when you believe this thought. Where do they fall on your Body Compass? Is it on the negative side? Great, let's choose this thought to work with a little.

First take the thought, and find out if it's true. It might feel very, very true. But is it true in the same way that we need oxygen to breathe and water to live?

Then start to notice what happens when you believe the thought. You've already noted the physical sensations, but what else happens? How do you treat the people around you? How do you treat yourself?

Now ask yourself what would happen if you were physically incapable of thinking the thought that brings you pain. If it was surgically removed from your brain, who is the person you would be if you couldn't think that thought? How does it feel in your body? How do you treat yourself and the people around you?

Once you've answered all those questions, what would be the opposite of your original thought? Can you think of three pieces of evidence proving why the opposite might be just as true as the original?

Listen for Messages, aka the Song Angel

I have never suffered major or clinical depression. But I have wondered how could what I was experiencing be all there is to life, to being on this vast and beautiful earth. There had to be something more than just paying rent and feeling mediocrely about everything. Back when I was in Life Coach Training, we learned about a concept called the Song Angel. The idea being sometimes, when the Universe is trying to deliver you a message but you're just not picking up on it, it's forced to get creative about its delivery systems. And sure enough, it did.

For me, it came in the form of Jay Z's "*This Can't Be Life.*" Definitely a vehicle I never could have anticipated. But I was floored in its accuracy and effectiveness. It was everything I felt. The lyrics killed me. "This can't be life, this can't be love/This can't be right, there's gotta be more, this can't be us." Which is what I was feeling. Like, verbatim. We are not put here to exist. We are put here to thrive. That has to be true. This can't be all that life is about. Yes, there is pizza and Tina Fey and coffee and the ocean. Life is so, so good. We are so, so blessed. But there had to be more. We were not put on earth to feel like this.

Notice what songs you're listening to a lot lately. I wonder if there's one that will jump out at you.

Follow Your Obsessions – No Matter How Random, Unlikely, or Seemingly Pointless

When *The Mindy Project* came out, I prepared myself to be a huge fan. Since I'm a lover of Mindy Kaling, women writers/ storytellers, and comedy, it seemed like a no-brainer. Week after week, I watched. Rooting for it hard, but never really loving it as much as I wanted to. No matter, I kept watching. Three seasons past, and I supported it, but that was pretty much it.

Fast forward to the next summer, I had a craving to watch *The Mindy Project*. It was a little strange considering that I hadn't, like, *loved* it the first time around, but I'm also a serial re-watcher, so it wasn't too crazy. I just assumed it was me being mildly diplomatic with myself (and with Mindy) and now I was giving us all a second chance.

In short, I became obsessed. I blew through episodes with a fervor that was kind of weird. I liked it more than was logical. All of a sudden, I LOVED *The Mindy Project*. I laughed. I let autoplay do its thing and lead me through four, five, six episodes at a time. (I figured six episodes was sort of the same length as a movie. Right?) I ignored my friends. I watched more episodes. Something had obviously changed.

Mindy became a role model for me. At first I became obsessed with her clothing (that Vivienne Westwood star jumpsuit? Shout out to Salvador Perez, the show's costume designer) but it was also more than that. I wanted to live like Mindy. Speak my mind. Make mistakes. Wear fun, beautiful clothes. Not be afraid of what other people thought. Make even more mistakes. Trust that the things that needed to land would land, and everything else would fade away. Have a blind confidence in myself and a vision of my own perfection that no one could touch. Almost irresponsibly think I could do no wrong. Make really insane mistakes. Be blatantly and unapologetically on my own team. Make a ton more mistakes, but at least have so much fun making them. Clothes like a piñata. Chanel bags in every color. Being bold, brash, and unapologetic. Because life is short, so why not?

I was not obsessed forever. But the timing could not have been an accident. *The Mindy Project* was a model for how to get back on my own team. To support my decisions. To live large and not apologize for the choices I was making. To make huge mistakes because it meant I was trying. To not apologize for living my life, however it looked. No, I do not believe that was an accident.

Also, over the course of writing this book, I was introduced to a concept called "golden-tongued wisdom." It's similar to a concept we've already talked about, the Song Angel. Imagine that for some reason the Universe is trying to get a message to you and it's gone through all the usual channels, but you haven't picked up on it yet. So it starts to get creative. It uses the songs you're listening to. It uses the shows on Netflix or Hulu. It shouts from the newspapers or podcasts. It's just trying to change the method of delivery so it actually gets to its intended receiver.

The Mindy Project was that for me. A message being sent in a form I could understand. Now this is not to say all your Netflix marathons are helpful. There is a clear line between numbing activities and those that make you feel more alive. Mindy Lahiri showed up at a time when I needed a model for the future – a hyper-confident woman who made mistakes by the second, barreled on forward, didn't apologize, and did it all while looking amazing and being super-awesome at her job. And then I got to reinforce this over and over again because there were multiple seasons. Maybe guidance is really everywhere. Maybe it does reveal itself in forms that make sense for you. Maybe sometimes it just doesn't have to be that deep.

Now, it's your turn. What have you been listening to, watching, obsessed with lately? Do any of them feel like they're really hitting home or sound similar to things you're going through? Any potential metaphors? You don't have to go digging or make meaning out of every tiny thing, but maybe just see what's out there. What's coming up for you? Maybe it's not actually a coincidence.

You Do Not Need to Be Like Everybody: Be the Awkward Weird One

If you are following your Body Compass, and making decisions solely based on things you want to try and explore, you will run the risk of being awkward, strange, or different. And that might feel crazy or scary or lonely. It might be harder when you've been raised in a community that claims (and is probably very well-meaning in their intention) to have your best interests at heart. But who might not if they knew what it was that you really wanted.

Take Mark. He went to business school despite a long history in the medical profession. Because the thought of graduating from business school and having an MBA made him feel like a baller. That was reason enough for him. None of his friends understood (he'd never given any indication he was interested in business until a few of his friends went to business school); his family was supportive, but hesitant. The thing is, business school made him feel like the most professional version of himself, it was a good challenge, and he knew it was something he would never regret. So he applied, was accepted, and enrolled.

After he graduated, he took a job in marketing for a pharmaceutical company. He'd never worked in anything close to marketing before, but they flipped over his medical and business history. His resume was by far the most impressive they'd seen of all the candidates they'd considered for his position. He's been promoted several times since. All because he did the thing that didn't make that much sense on paper, didn't make sense for the people around him, but made perfect sense for him. It wasn't easy, but he knew how suffocating it felt to do things simply for how they looked to other people.

Do Everything Wrong; Make All the Mistakes. Because Why Not?

When we're stuck and lost and unhappy, we often look for the one perfect decision that will make everything right again. I cannot tell you how many clients I have worked with that wish for the *one thing* that would make everything better, give them the answer, or fix it all. Whether it's a test that would tell them what they're really good at, or the perfect job so they can finally stop thinking about what they want to do with their lives, they are looking for one answer. And the pressure they put on that decision isn't fair. How can anyone make just one decision that also happens to be the decision that solves everything? You can't, so don't even try. Instead of putting undue pressure on the right decision, what if we just thought about the next right decision, knowing there will be others, and knowing they can all be changed? Don't dwell. Dwelling leads to stagnancy and stagnancy leads to self-loathing. Just make something, or try something, or quit something, and then move on to the next thing. Try. Take a very small risk. Just make one decision.

My client Shannon almost became a long-distance truck driver because she just wanted to make one decision rather than live with another second of ambiguity. She was ready to make something work no matter what she needed to do, and she was ready to have that decision over and done with. (Note: She did not become a long-distance trucker.)

There's always a first decision. And if it's been weeks/ months/years since you've made a decision, then it becomes totally understandable why you might think you need to put all the eggs of that decision in one basket. But, here's the thing.

Immediately after that decision, you will need to make a second decision. And then not too long after the second decision, you will need to make a third. And if we're really being honest here, there will probably be a few more after that. So please, please, please, don't think about that "one decision" that will fix everything. Just think about the next best decision. And then the next best one after that. And then the one after that. Because there will always be more. Very few things in life are unfixable. Just keep making decisions. Just keep it moving. Don't be so precious with your decisions. There will be plenty more of them to make and 90% of everything is fixable.

Remember, none of this will kill you. It's all part of the plan. If you want to be brave and strong, these are the things that will make you brave and strong. They never get easier. Ever. The people who tell you it gets easier are lying. But you become more used to what resistance feels like. You get more used to gearing yourself up to leap. You get more used to what it will feel like if you *don't* do it. Yes, you might be scared. But you'll be even madder if you let the fear win.

Something to Try: Is There a Message Trying to Reach You?

Identify one thought that might be giving you a hard time. Challenge it the way I've outlined in this chapter. Also, think about what you've been consuming lately in terms of books, shows, music, etc. Is there anything that jumps out at you that might be helpful?

For more exercises, recordings, and pretty worksheets, hop over to sarakravitz.com/toolkit and download the toolkit now!

Chapter 4

Movement vs. Stagnancy & Stagnancy vs. Stillness

"You must do the thing you think you cannot do."

Eleanor Roosevelt

The goal of giving you lots of ways to check in with your body in addition to finding out things you think you shouldn't want (but do) is to start moving you toward getting those things. Generating a list is great. It's necessary and it does require time and attention. It's also good to spend some time drilling down into any specifics that might make initiating an action easier or harder. But eventually the time comes for you to act.

For some of us it's very easy to spend the majority of our time and efforts focused on hammering out the "right" list and identifying the "right" actions to the point that we never take a single first step. The Body Compass will help give you an idea of where to go. Your jealousy will do the same. But ultimately, it is you that has to make stuff happen. You can trust that this will be uncomfortable. You can trust that you, a grown-ass person, might have an actual tantrum (spoken from experience). That just means you're doing everything perfectly.

The Awkwardness Begins

Before I became a life coach, back when I was still proving I COULD MAKE THINGS WORK DAMMIT, I was lucky enough to be on an insurance plan that was fairly committed to preventative care. It was one of those typical, but frequent, phases I would go through where I thought something was wrong with me because everyone knew what they wanted to do except me. They were all working hard and advancing in the world, and here I was, older than I'd ever been, and absolutely none the wiser. I was constantly berating myself for not "having this figured out by now," and feeling like I wanted to work really hard and be proud of myself, but never knowing how to take the first step. I knew something was off, and I knew I had to get other people involved, but I had no idea where to start. So, I made an appointment with a Licensed Clinical Social Worker (LCSW) through my health insurance just to get the ball rolling. I felt stuck and crazy and like I was just cycling through the same garbage over and over again. Super fun, I know. So I decided to bring in a professional.

Immediately after meeting with the (LCSW), I registered with a group that would be going through *The Artist's Way* together, and committed to several sessions of a version of dance therapy. Those two things may not have changed everything, but I can say with absolute certainty that nothing would have changed without them.

The Aha Moment: Do Everything Wrong. Make All the Mistakes. Get Happy.

Outside of the actual therapeutic benefits of dance therapy, just the process of walking in the door, taking off your shoes, and living through the five minutes before it begins, is truly its own kind of therapy. Dance therapy, for those who don't know, looks at the correlation between movement and emotion. As the participant, it's when someone puts on music and gives you dance prompts. Then you follow them, and afterwards you discuss what came up for you. Just being able to dance in front of a stranger, on command, is an exercise in... something. For people like me who are controlling (to put it mildly) and have anxiety about being seen and judged, just this part is a huge challenge. But I also truly believe that once you identify something you are scared of, you have to do that thing. It wasn't the kind of activity I was repulsed or revolted by. It didn't feel heavy or gross or like I really didn't want to do it. It felt like pure fear. Like I was just scared. *Really* scared. I could also tell that the only thing I was afraid of was feeling or looking stupid, which really meant that the only thing that was scared here was my ego. And that's exactly why I knew I had to do it. Because the fear of looking stupid is simply not a good enough reason not to do something.

We all need constant evidence that reminds us how brave we can be. If we don't do the thing we're scared of, it will just show up somewhere else. I also believe it's better to understand why we're afraid of something rather than be held hostage by that fear. Dancing in front of an intently watching stranger was the terrifying challenge in front of me, so dancing in front of a stranger it was going to be.

And Holy Lord was it terrifying. But it was also one of the best things I've ever done for myself. Each and every terrifying second. I remember the resistance, both physical and emotional, before almost every session. The moments leading up to the sessions. The extreme feeling of, "I don't want to do this." The almost mini-tantrum about to happen because my body was so not okay with the unknown that was in front of it. The physical sensations of panic, the fear of not knowing, of looking stupid, of being unsure. This never went away. It happened every single time.

But then I would start.

Because at a certain point, there's a split second's worth of hesitation in your resistance, and you just begin. And then you're doing it. And you can always stop, but you know something inside you will die if you do.

I would try and stay present. Because after all, I was there. I was doing it. Sometimes, in the beginning, before it would start, I would have to compartmentalize a little just to keep myself in the room. Because the anticipation could be so intimidating, separating myself from the fact that the body doing this was mine was helpful. I would think "Why not get something out of this," a calm and rational conclusion from someone who also happened to be simultaneously freaking out. But it would work. I always stayed, and I always benefitted.

During the process, things would come up. Sometimes almost immediately. And that's how I knew it was worth doing again. Messages that my hyper-verbal, overactive brain wouldn't let through were finally allowed to have their moment. It served as an access tool – exactly like the Body Compass from Chapter 2. It's part of the gift of having a body. Even when you think your brain doesn't know what you want or how you feel, your body does – so create as many opportunities as possible for your body to speak to you. It absolutely never got easier, but I had more and more proven examples of why it was worth the discomfort, and why I should keep doing it. I never died from it (!), and I always learned something.

Dancing in the Dark

The most important lesson I learned from dance therapy was: "Don't be afraid of the dark. It's where the most fun is." One particular exercise was to switch back and forth between dancing in the light and in the dark, and between dancing "well" and dancing "poorly." Once I got over my initial awkwardness and limitations of my technical dance skills, it became clear how fun it was to dance "in the dark." (That's both literal and a metaphor. Sometimes my eyes were closed.) I noticed I wasn't afraid of making mistakes in the dark. I was already so bad that I couldn't make it any worse. It didn't matter. Which in turn made it kind of fun.

When I was dancing "in the light" and dancing "well," there was all this pressure to not make mistakes and to be "good." And of course, I had limited "good" movements because the others were "bad." So in addition to the pressure of being good, it was also kind of boring. Once I did my five or six "good" moves, there wasn't really anything left to do. Whereas in the dark, I had a full range. I could do whatever I wanted. And that immediately made it more fun and subsequently "good."

This made me think about what else I might be missing while I was too busy worrying about being "good." What was being afraid of the dark costing me? What about all the fun things I hadn't tried yet, or even thought of to try? Were there things I could even be good at, but assumed otherwise? During the exercise, I was freed to think in ways I hadn't been allowing myself. I was able to go places and try things I never would have with my limited ideas about what I assumed was "good." And, of course, ironically enough, these things would end up being actually better than my "good" things.

Piercing the Armor

Of course it never would have happened if my witness, the person guiding me through these exercises, hadn't been tremendously loving and kind. Any hint of judgment would have sent me out of there so fast, and this would be a book about the racket that is dance therapy. But that's also another lesson. One that well-known author and academic Brené Brown has a whole lot more insightful things to say about than I do. She writes about only being vulnerable with the people who have earned it. But if somehow a hater gets through and finds their way into your inner circle, keep it moving. (I may be paraphrasing here.) Let them live in their sad, angry, bitter existence. Do not let the person who is dragging you down to make themselves feel better affect a single thing you do. You're the brave one. You're the one who actually did something – not just sat idly by watching people make real attempts to better their lives. Remember, they're just jealous, and they only wish they could be brave and do what you are doing.

Look Forward to Being Bad at Things

So many of my clients are afraid of being "bad" at things. I had one client who was so afraid of doing something wrong that she almost didn't quit her job. Because she was afraid she would be bad at the next job. She was afraid of all the things she assumed she didn't know. So she was almost willing to stay at the job she hated because she believed she was "good" at it. She was willing to hate her life for the next however many years rather than risk being bad at something. Believe me, I get it. But is it really a way to live?

We were able to question her fear of being bad at something. What was the worst that could happen? She could make a mistake in front of everyone and then everyone would know she had made a mistake. Her credibility would be shot forever, and she may as well quit that job too. She realized that if her best friend or a fellow co-worker had done that, she would have thought it was unnecessary and basically insane, but yet she expected herself to be perfect at all times.

We thought of previous times in her life when she hadn't known exactly how to do everything when she started, but was able to figure it out over time, and be successful over time. She had a proven track record in her life of these exact circumstances, and she had succeeded. This was no different. She knew enough to get started and she would learn the rest as she went through the process because that's what she had done before. And she did. She quit her job and started a new one that she was very excited about. Totally nervous, but excited about her bravery and the change she was able to make.

How Do You Know the Difference Between Resistance That's Good and Resistance That's Bad?

None of the exercises in this chapter are effortless. None of them feel, or felt, like ease. Maybe eventually. One day. Far into the future. But I have yet to experience that. The moments leading up to them can range from terror to anger, and there's almost always resistance. Most notably, I felt physical resistance. I experienced a buildup in my chest I was sure would turn into an outburst similar to a child's tantrum. There was very little grace or dignity going on in my body. I wanted the change that would come from being there. I wanted the feeling that comes at the end of doing really good, really hard work. There were plenty of moments in between that were *hard*. But once I crossed the threshold, all was different. The moment right before, I was at my most worked up and I felt like I didn't want to do this thing so much that I was about to cry or panic. But then I started, and that feeling almost immediately dissipated.

Consumption vs. Production

We are a consumer culture. We consume media, GIFs, ice cream, Beyoncé albums. The opposite of consumption is production. Those who spend all day consuming and no time producing feel imbalanced. Because we are made to produce. And that is why Elizabeth Gilbert's *Big Magic* is so brilliant.

She tells us to produce anything. Just make something because you can. Because you want to. It doesn't have to be epic, or maybe it will be epic. Who knows? Because you haven't made it yet. Make a terrible collage, or a reductionist painting. Do it because it's different from what you normally do, and that's reason enough. Draw your dark side. Write a letter to your dark side. Write a saga about coming back from the dark side. We are alone on the dark side – until we are not. Let someone know they are not alone.

Processing the Darkness

Sometimes we need additional modes and methods to process the darkness. The goal is motion – cycling through thoughts, so they don't have time to take root and convince you they are the thought that is, in fact, the truth. And sometimes we are so sure how we think about things is the correct, or only way that we need something new to help us process what's happening. That's why art is important. Maybe you can't totally explain how you're feeling, but you see something or read something that articulates it. And now you can understand it more – both the situation and yourself. I don't just mean art in the fussy sense. We're not just talking about museums and sculpture and finished pieces. Of course, these are part of it. Paintings in museums, albums of music, books to read – these are all powerful tools we can enlist to help us process the dark side. It also helps that so many of these are non-verbal. Sometimes what we need to express can't be said, or explained. It's a feeling. And sometimes we need non-verbal tools to help us get through the feelings.

The goal of these aides is to help get any stagnant emotions moving. One suggestion is music. Music can be really powerful for this. Music can help build the bridge between you and your emotions. And you don't have to make anything or travel to a gallery. Listening to sad songs or angry songs might feel contradictory or fatalistic, but it's fine. It's great actually. If it's helping you to feel your emotions as opposed to suppressing them, let's do it. We want to honor our emotions fully here. We want to feel them fully. Inhabit them in their totality. Get comfortable in your sadness or anger or however it is that you feel. Show it that it's welcome here. We are no longer afraid of it, and we want it to feel welcome. It's been trying to get our attention for so long, and now we are finally giving it center stage. It just wants to be seen. It doesn't want to be ignored. Not in a pushy, arrogant way, but in a scared, lonely child kind of way. If you knew your sadness was just a sad, scared, lonely six-year-old, would you lock your door and turn off the lights? Or would you invite it in, wrap it in blankets, feed it cookies, and hold it until it wasn't sad anymore? That's what your emotions are. They're not out to get you. They're not trying to bring you down. They just want to be loved. They just want to be held.

You read the above and think, "Oh, okay. I'll let in a six-year old"... sounds great! One question – um, how? Music (or art or dance) can help with that. It can help the two of you meet each other, get acquainted, and start to learn the same language. It might not even take that long. Internally, you might not even know how queued up you are to feel these feelings. One song and it might all be right there. Or you might have done a really good job burying the sadness. You might know all the ways it tries to sneak out, so you have extra locks and a guard dog and an alarm system and a cop car outside of the house. It might take longer. In that case, you don't need to fake anything. If sad songs don't do it for you, don't listen to "sad" songs. Try Christmas songs (I'm listening to them right now – they help me write) or songs you used to listen to as a kid (80s hair bands are another favorite of mine).

Listening to music that doesn't allow you to process emotions in a practiced way can be helpful. Because Christmas is such a short time (even though it never feels that way at the time, amirite?) and during childhood, we often didn't have the tools to outsmart emotions in very sophisticated ways. That can help when we're trying to process them later on.

Giving Yourself Space to Wade Through the Dark Side

At the last real-ish job I had, one of the silver linings came in the most unexpected form, as they are wont to do. There was one early morning task that no one really wanted, but it happened almost daily, so we (the other co-workers and I) would rotate it accordingly. It wasn't totally fair to ask one person to come in significantly earlier every day, so we would share. But soon, I started volunteering more often than not. It was a fairly simple job, and there's something amazing about waking up early in NYC and commuting before prime commuting time (when it's actually tolerable). In addition to those small but not insignificant perks, there was one surprise one. This is the one that kept me volunteering for this early morning task.

Once the task was over, there was a relatively long waiting period in a very quiet place where practically no one ever went.

THIS was the gold. After completing the first part, I was granted a minimum of one hour of silence in a sleepy, dark, quiet room. For many of my co-workers, this was less than ideal. An hour of sitting alone with nothing to do. I not only relished this time, but I actively chased it. A quiet, uninterrupted hour was a precious resource. It was here that I could write, with little to no interruptions, for an hour. Or read for an hour. Or sit in quiet contemplation. It was a little window of peace right at the onset of my day. A true blessing. In a world with so much noise, and so many things competing for attention, here was the gift of an hour of solitude. #blessed. When the job ended, I wrote these words, "Strangely enough, I might just miss that waiting room the most. That dark, quiet, peaceful area where the quiet sunk through to your bones and just sitting there felt wonderful. Held and sleepy and wonderful."

My wish for you is a place like that. A place where you feel held and sleepy and wonderful. It was there that I could write Morning Pages (second mention of this book – that's how much I think you should read it, *The Artist's Way* by Julia Cameron, recommends Morning Pages, which is the act of free-writing three pages first thing in the morning to basically empty your brain of all the garbage floating around to ready your headspace for your work ahead). Or I could write random attempts at essays or other random musings that I had no idea where they were going or what they might turn into. (Shout out to this book!) Sometimes I read, and other times I meditated, but most of the time I wrote. It was such a great low-stakes opportunity to write at a time when I was judging myself harshly. Here was some time to write, and it would always end. And I would immediately get back to work and forget every word I had just written. Perfect.

Of course now I can look back at it and see that it actually *was* perfect. At the time there was a lot of angst that I was settling for a stupid job and not fulfilling my potential and wasting even more time. Putting other people's needs and wants before mine, but also not even knowing what my needs and wants were. That's why trusting the feeling of that space was so important. It was peaceful and content and luxurious in its silence and stolen-ness. Like I was stealing time for myself amidst the real world.

Use Your Body Compass

Here's where that great tool from Chapter 2 comes in handy. It's all just basically an epic game of Warmer/Colder. Outside the social reckoning of the mind, the body responds to what it wants. It gravitates toward more of what you want by showing up as peaceful, calm, spacious feelings in the body. Things I don't want or am forcing myself to want because I think I should want them, have a more constricting quality to them. Does the thing in front of me make me feel more gross, or more relieved? Does it make me feel heavier and more weighed down? Or does it make me feel freer? Here's where you can use the Body Compass you calibrated. What did you name the associations attached to your negative and positive physical sensations? This is a perfect time to enlist them.

How do I know the difference? Because I know I want to write. I want to coach people. I know I want these things. And yet sometimes I don't want to *do* these things. I want them but I'm scared of being bad at them. Scared that the truth is that I'm a terrible writer, or will never be a good enough coach. That's how I know they're for me. It's not the process I'm afraid of – it's the outcome. The fear is just pushing me back to where it's safe. Where people haven't been able to laugh at me yet. Where people haven't judged me yet. It's not guiding me away from any of the actual work it takes to do these things.

Conversely, I'm not scared of never getting into law school. I'm repulsed by what might happen if I ever did get into law school. I'm not scared of the long road to being a lawyer; I'm scared of actually *being* a lawyer. I feel physical resistance to those logic puzzles they make you do. However, when you tell me I'm allowed to write another book, I want to clap my hands (even though I'm well aware of what the process of writing a book is like). That's my Body Compass in action. What's yours like?

My Yoga Story (That Will Definitely Not Be Everyone's Yoga Story)

I'm not just plugging yoga because this is a self-help book and I am a life coach. I am a huge advocate of physical activity that forces the chatter of your mind to shut off for at least a little while, so your body can have a minute to show you that it knows a thing or two (see above section on Dance Therapy). While Dance Therapy probably had a more significant impact over a much shorter period, yoga was my go-to for years.

I was at a job that I hated. Like, cried every Sunday night, was angry almost all the time, straight up HATED. And I knew I should be doing yoga. It was just one of those things that you know, deep down in the fibers of your being. Even though I just knew it was something I needed to be doing, I had no idea how to just walk into a yoga studio. Luckily, I had a friend who always seemed to know what to do. So she took me to a yoga class. Then I went again without her. And then I started going four to five times a week.

Yoga served several purposes. First, it taught me how to spend 90 minutes not being angry and not thinking about anything other than what I was physically doing at the time. Want to fall out of a pose? Think about that infuriating thing your boss did earlier that day, or the client you want to murder. It taught me to shut my brain off and get some perspective. Second, it taught me about the concept of surrender. This is its own separate book, but getting into child's pose and saying "I surrender" is deep. Like, *deep*. When you're in a situation you hate, learning to surrender is big. Trust. When you're angry or frustrated, just try surrendering. It's different from "let it go," which is a well-meaning, well-intentioned phrase that is certainly helpful, but different from straight-up surrendering. Letting go is releasing; surrendering is accepting. One allows you to rid yourself of a burden, the other allows you to accept something that exists just as it is, without changing it at all. Just say them both out loud, and see if you have a different physical reaction to each. Third, yoga is where I learned that "everything that happened today is gone. It's over and it's not coming back. So bring yourself back to the present moment."

Real talk for a minute: the kink in this plan is that a lot of yoga is terrible these days (if you've tried yoga and didn't like it, it probably wasn't you. It was probably terrible.) I was very lucky to be handed a magical studio run by three geniuses who were well-versed in all aspects of yoga. I'm aware of the garbage that's out there, so if you're down on yoga or having a hard time finding a studio, I get it. I was very lucky to walk into the studio I did. The only thing I can offer is that it's worth doing the work to find someone or someplace you connect with (this applies to any physical activity, not just yoga). I know yoga's not for everyone, but it's a physical practice that gets you out of your head. In our logic-heavy, reason-oriented society, that's a gift. So just think about it. (Ditto for the dance therapy.)

Just Do Something

This book happened because I really understood that at some point you just need words on a page. That's what a book is. We can have a philosophical conversation about what a book is, what a story is, how e-books play into it, the difference between a book and a good book, but the bottom line is words. Lots and lots of words on lots and lots of pages. Without them, you have nothing. Putting words on a page, and trusting that many of those words will be ones you haven't thought of yet, is key. Sometimes it's writing words you didn't know you felt because your brain is taking you somewhere you hadn't planned on, and then deleting a lot of those words because your brain took you to a place that wasn't really the point. So sometimes it pays to not place too much value on each and every one of them. Some will stick, some will get deleted, but you can't get to the next word until you write the first one down.

Doing something, starting somewhere, doesn't have to be nothing, but it doesn't have to be everything. Just begin, learn a little by doing, course correct, do more, learn more, change everything, but keep going – see how starting shows you a lot more than endless planning.

Something to Try: Do Something

Pick one activity that is movement oriented. Give your brain a chance to rest. Try yoga, dance, Pilates, running – yes, it will probably be awkward. But give it a shot. Take notes about how you feel before. Take notes on how you feel afterwards. Is there a difference?

For more exercises, recordings, and pretty worksheets, hop over to sarakravitz.com/toolkit and download the toolkit now!

Chapter 5

The Easiest, Most Glam
Version of Your Life

"Just as we can know the ocean because it always tastes of salt, we can recognize enlightenment because it always tastes of freedom."
Buddha

You Might Feel Stupid About the Thing You Want

One of the most annoying things that ever happened to me was that I became a life coach. I really did not see that coming. I mean, I did, but I didn't. I thought maybe I would be a therapist. I imagined it would become a Woody Allen movie. I would live in an Upper West Side apartment teaming with books and plants. I would spend all day talking with women about their lives. And it would be called therapy – a respectable, very accepted, and intelligent-sounding profession. I was very sure this would happen. I enrolled in a Masters of Social Work program and started school, certain this would be the fastest, easiest route to my new life in a non-embarrassing job.

And then everything changed.

The year I started school, all of a sudden you had to accrue 3,000 work hours to be able to sit for your licensing exam. Which, I guess, would be fine if you actually wanted to be a social worker. The problem was I was using this as a workaround to avoid ten more years of school. And maybe enough of us had done this that they were finally catching on, but I was doing this because I thought I could go to school for two years, sit for the exam, and BAM! Therapist.

Yes, that is correct. It was too easy.

So now my two-year plan was becoming a five-year plan. Which, like, fine. Again, maybe not a problem if you liked social work, or school, or other things involved in this process. But I did not. This was supposed to be my shortcut and it was becoming very not short.

I actually didn't mind the school part. I love school. For me, it's so much easier than life. Someone just gives you a list of things to do and read, and you do them and read them. You meet once a week and have an interesting conversation about them. What could be bad?

Apparently, things. Things could be bad.

One of my graduate-level classes was full of people who didn't know what gentrification was. When I tried to switch my placement, there was a meeting where I had to act as a referee between two grown, professional women, trained as social workers, who were supposed to be helping me, but were really just yelling at each other. We had to write out sessions with clients so that we could discuss them with our supervisors. These write-ups were very, very long. I could never totally remember what happened during my sessions, so I would make most of it up. (Don't judge me.)

The other key element of this plan was that I actually enjoy social work school, which was not turning out to be the case. It was fairly easy, which was great. And I actually learned a lot of things I still think about today. But after one semester, I had had my fill. Plus, school was expensive, and the starting salary of a social worker just did not seem like enough. So I quit after one semester.

Point being: life coach it was going to be. An email landed in my inbox around the time I started thinking about quitting from a life coach whose books I loved. She had created a training for life coaches, and it covered things I actually wanted to be working on. (Another side note: in my semester at social work school, I learned that I didn't want to work in any of the areas that would be covered.) The schedule of classes was manageable, and we would be doing hands-on work throughout the training.

It was all shaping up nicely. The catch was it was life coaching. I had to look people in the eye and tell them I was a professional coacher of life. WTF?

Just how basic and cheesy are we going for?! Should we just throw in a pumpkin spice latte and a pairs of Uggs?! (I deeply love both those things, BTW.) So I guess I'm basic and cheesy. Oh well. I wasn't really going to be able to hide it forever and have a happy, successful life. I choose happy, successful life. I hope you do the same. Yes, I might be a basic, but there's a lot of basic stuff that's awesome. So I'm good.

Build a Life of Quality; Do Not Settle for Mediocrity

Do not apologize for who you are or what you want. If you are doing something you do not love but know is temporary, or are getting something out of it, that's fine. That's great even. It's great that you are in motion. One of my best friends once said, "It's really hard to get going once you stop completely." And for the people who needed to hear that, that's for you. If you know that quitting your job with nothing on the horizon will send you into a spiral of fear and paralysis, do not quit your job. If you know that you will not be able to fully pursue your next steps without leaving your current situation, quit your job. If you don't know, do one. And then the other. It's not a perfect system. You might pick the wrong one. But it will really be the right one.

One of my clients switched jobs. She was happy because she had spent so much time weighing her decision, mulling over the pros and cons, and generally worrying about pulling the trigger. But now all that was over. She had made a decision! And it was a good one! Now she could kick back and finally enjoy her life. Cue the applause.

Three months later, her outlook was less positive. So we worked through why she thought she had made the wrong decision. Was it that she made a mistake? Did she ignore her intuition? Was she desperate to solve this problem, so she went for the first opportunity that came her way?

Spoiler alert: it was none of these things. She made the best decision she could with the information she had at the time. Then, it turned out the situation was different than what was promised. She chose to start looking again, and within a few months she had a new job. It was just something that happened, and she chose to do something about it. It didn't mean she made the wrong choice, or didn't really know herself, or didn't have a bliss. It just meant her new boss was a huge liability and she had the sense to start planning her exit before things got really bad. Sometimes things just happen! It doesn't mean it's not frustrating or deflating. Of course is it. But it also can be relegated, fairly quickly, to the past.

YOLO Is an Existing Phenomenon, So Why Not Use It?

Living a life worried about what people think is stupid. It's certainly more stupid that any of the things you might think are too stupid to pursue. Yes, your ridiculous, embarrassing, nothing thing that you want to do is worth it. Yes, you have to tell people about it. No, they will not care. Yes, they will laugh at you. And then they will remember they need to buy milk, and move on with their lives. We will all move on with our lives.

Don't be afraid to want what you want. Make a declarative statement. Add YOLO after it. You'll know if you don't want it.

The More Frivolous, the Better

Get excited about your life. This doesn't have to be the part where you revamp everything. Instead, start to introduce little things. For me, it was getting lattes every day, getting weekly-ish manicures, and buying cute writing instruments so I would be excited to write every day. That was it. Coffee, manicures, pens. Not too crazy and totally frivolous. Even when I didn't have the money, I still did these things. I called them the price of sanity. Because your life has to have beauty and excitement, and sometimes it's easier to start small. (Update: now there's a rainbow sweatshirt and an iridescent wallet that I want. See? The more frivolous the better.)

Don't Be in Such a Rush

Sometimes you give things away and sometimes they are taken away. Either way there is now space. Fill that space or don't. But do it intentionally. If you've identified something you're tolerating, there's no need to rush to replace that thing. Also, you don't always need an explanation to change something. "I don't like this anymore" is a perfectly good reason. So is "because I wanted to."

Add Beauty In

"People are drawn to beauty," said my friend Zoe one day almost 20 years ago. "God don't make ugly and God don't like ugly," said *The Divine Secrets of the YaYa Sisterhood*. Art, flowers, beautiful clothes, good light, functional design – we are drawn to these things. It's not superficial. It's part of our birthright. We may all think that different things are beautiful, but we are all drawn to beautiful things. So surround yourself with them. Fill up your life with them. Does it seem ridiculous? Maybe it's more ridiculous not to.

What are the things you do to make the world more beautiful? What are your tiny offerings to the light? A sequined sweatshirt? A beautifully framed letter that means something to you? They might seem insignificant, but they are serious and they mean something. You are adding to the beauty of the universe. Not because these are superficially aesthetically pleasing things to look at. But because they are things that inspire smiles. If they make you feel good, they infuse you with an energy that gets transmitted to other people. It spreads. And it's all genuine.

I remember reading a *Top Shelf* interview featured on the blog *Into the Gloss* about this woman who was a counselor of victims of domestic violence. She said, "I take care of others on a daily basis, and I firmly believe that in order to care for others you must care for yourself." PREACH. Of course it's another way of saying what women have heard for years when they were finally kind of allowed to start including themselves in the list of people they take care of on a daily basis. It's another way of reminding ourselves that we can't take care of other people unless we take care of ourselves. And sometimes it's good to remember just how key that is.

Make yourself such a fan of your own life that everything else is a bonus. What people do, or don't do, for you doesn't matter because you've already taken care of yourself. This is not to say we don't need anyone and we should all forge our lives alone. But if you're already focused on making yourself really happy, you might be less angry at your partner when they can't read your mind. Or your friend who keeps talking about herself. Or your boss who hasn't given you any positive feedback in a while. Give yourself all the love. Give yourself all the presents. Learn everything you can about yourself: what you want, what you need, what makes you happy. And then start checking off that list. But make your life so ridiculously beautiful that there's a rainbow cape of protection that's draped around your shoulders and just watch how the negativity rolls off you all day. Be the light no matter what kind of darkness surrounds you.

You Have to Be All in on Your Own Life

You can't pooh-pooh yourself or hide behind a wall of cynicism or sarcasm. Certainly not because the thing you want and are not letting yourself have might be cheesy. You have to let yourself feel each feeling and cherish every one of them. Honor them. Even if you don't tell the world about them, you have to tell yourself about them. You have to tell yourself and not laugh at them.

You can't laugh at what you want. Or laugh hard, but don't belittle it. Protect it at all costs. People who don't have the guts to admit what they want are going to come for it. They are going to use it to justify why they are not protecting the thing they want. Do not let them. Your bravery does not come at the cost of their life choices. It is not your job to affirm anyone's life choices but your own. Be on your own team; no one else will do it for you. There will be times when you are the only one who understands something or thinks it's a good idea. It might be lonely; you might feel misunderstood. Be all in anyway.

Also, maybe it's not your *dream*. Maybe it's not EVERYTHING YOU'VE EVER WANTED. But maybe it's something you have to do to get to the next place. Maybe it's something you have to do to take care of yourself so you can go into the world and take yourself seriously.

Tami Taylor-ing = Life Hack

If you've never seen the television show, *Friday Night Lights*, this next section will be lost on you. But that also means you should put this book down immediately and go watch it. (Maybe I'll join you? Also, you're welcome. Texas forever, y'all.) If the only thing you get out of this book is having watched *Friday Night Lights*, it will all have been worth it.

Anyway, somewhere along the line, I learned that whenever I was uncomfortable about going into a situation, maybe because it was new or something I was subtly dreading, I would invoke Tami Taylor and all would be well. Tami Taylor (in the vast majority of situations – no one, even her, is perfect) is the respectable, respectful, strong, and eloquent human I would like to come across as during most moments of my life. Tami Taylor-ing is essentially a super-specific, hyper-focused version of faking-it-until-you make-it.

Pretending to be Tami Taylor allowed me to get a handle on situations that were TBD while acting like the best version of myself. By channeling her, I could be assured I was acting in a way I could be proud of – or at least not totally mortified by – until my actual self caught up with the present moment.

Channeling my nervousness meant I could be assured I wasn't burdening the people around me with misdirected energy. I also knew that Tami Taylor would always be classy and never be crazy, so even when I couldn't trust my next step, I always knew what Tami would do. Does this sound psychotic? Maybe like something a washed-up actress might do? The answer to both of those questions is yes. However, it allowed me to engage in new situations in a way that helped me approximate feeling comfortable until I was *actually* comfortable.

Here's the thing: it works every time. But, like, every. time. Polite, but not self-sacrificing. Enthusiastic, but not false. Positive, but non-committal. Also, a southern accent helps (even if it's just in your head. Or not.). Once I had to give a presentation at 6am in front of 80 US soldiers with 10-ish hours' notice (eight of which I was asleep for). You might guess that I was nervous. You would be correct.

What did I do? I Tami Taylor-ed it. Like, down to a slight twang and even saying y'all. No one there knew I was born near Katz's Deli and have only been to Texas once. And no one gave me any weird looks after, either. Granted, most of them were probably asleep with their eyes open, but it didn't matter. I channeled my inner Tami Taylor and I won.

Try it. Or pick your own appropriate role model. It works in almost any scenario. It allows me to wear a suit of politeness, to exist in a state of deference without thinking I'm compromising everything I believe in. It allows me to be classy, but not crazy. It allows me to engage, but not self-sacrifice. Probably, most importantly, it allows me to observe and to witness by providing space to breathe in uncomfortable situations without physically leaving them, or checking out mentally. It's almost the equivalent of an invisibility cloak. I can be present physically while figuring out how I feel about a situation emotionally. Or allows it me to stick it out a few more minutes when all I want to do is bail, but my ride isn't ready to go.

Plus, it allows me the opportunity to be Mrs. Coach! And, let's be honest, to imagine a day in the life with that hair.

Something to Try: Feed the Best Version of Yourself

Identify three things you can bring into your life to make it feel more luxurious. It can be an activity or a physical object (or maybe even the removal of some objects). Exercise, reading, candles, writing, a phone date with someone you actually want to talk to, or maybe a few minutes planning your week and setting some intentions. Think of something that makes you feel like the highest functioning version of yourself. Now think of two more of those things, and spend some time doing them, or bringing them into your space.

For more exercises, recordings, and pretty worksheets, hop over to sarakravitz.com/toolkit and download the toolkit now!

Chapter 6

Letting Go of Even More Than You Thought

"If you hear a voice within you say 'you cannot paint,' then by all means paint, and that voice will be silenced."
Vincent Van Gogh

When "Yes to Life" Becomes "No" to Yourself

Let's be clear. I am a "Yes to Life" person. I like saying, "Yes and...." I believe Tina Fey, Amy Poehler, Bethenny Frankel, and my father when they exalt the party line and say things like, "Say yes. Figure it out later." I'm sure you've all heard about Tina Fey and Amy Poehler's life-philosophy-learned-via-improv-comedy: "Yes, and...." Skinnygirl Cocktails founder Bethenny Frankel (who clearly has done something right because not many people have a product they can sell for over $100 million dollars and three best-sellers) wrote a book called *A Place of Yes*. These are three women I will listen to, whole-heartedly and without objection, when they tell me to say yes to life.

And I think they would all agree with me when I say, you cannot say yes without saying no.

Hedging my bets with this answer? Possibly.

But let me explain.

I might have figured out I am a huge liar, like, three weeks ago. As you may have guessed, I say yes a lot. Mostly because I know that I am a person who regrets the things I don't do. I also know that I am terrible at initiating plans, so if I didn't say yes to the majority of my friends' invitations, I probably wouldn't have any friends. These two factors are probably the most significant forces behind my "yes to life" lifestyle. And yet, in writing this book, it has become pretty clear that saying yes a lot is also a way to not have to figure out what you want. It also makes you think you're not being negative. And apparently I have a fear of looking negative (dark side!). So I say yes a lot. Yes, to dinners, weddings, trips, things that on the surface seem perfectly pleasant (and to be fair, most are a lot of fun), but are ultimately compromises of myself.

FOMO

Friday night, staring down the barrel of a packed weekend of "fun" plans, used to make me feel terrible. All those seemingly fun plans felt like massive workouts - spending money I didn't have, expending energy that was fast depleting. I mean, obviously I should have been saying no to some of these very generous offers from some very well-meaning people who I legitimately enjoy spending time with.

Sometimes it's hard to rejecting perfectly wonderful offers for seemingly no reason.

Now we know a couple of things. First, FOMO. The Fear of Missing Out is real. The thing is (which I certainly didn't know, and might be kind of impossible to know as a twenty-something or a certain kind of person), when your own life is so awesome, there is nothing you can miss out on. That dinner? Was never your dinner to go to. That night alone? Make it awesome. Make it something you would never want to miss out on. Pick a wine, pick a movie, pick a meal, light a candle, buy a super-soft blanket. Clean your apartment before you settle in. Make it like a hotel (I love hotels – that might be too sterile for you, but hopefully you get the idea). Don't just flip channels and eat whatever. Give it some structure. Make it its own event. Treat yourself like someone you are trying to impress with a beautiful night in. Take pride in the care and effort you've made for yourself. Post an Instagram about it (remember, pics or it never happened. Kidding. Or not.) I don't care if it clutters the internet. I think we can already agree that ship has sailed.

Of course, there are times when you need to leave the house. It's necessary to engage with the world. No man is an island, etc. But the key is knowing when. Or at least giving yourself a decent shot at figuring out when.

And, of course, you'll get it wrong sometimes.

A dinner out with your crew that you would have thought would hit the spot might wind up being $50 more than you could afford. Or everyone is complaining when you're trying to focus on how you can be an agent of change in your own life. The trick is to not beat yourself up when you take a chance and it's not what you thought it would be. No, you shouldn't have known better. You made a decision based on the information you had at the time. Now, let it go. Yes, you have to listen to yourself, but sometimes the world is just the world. You couldn't possibly have known the outcome at the onset. Let's repeat that one and apply it to every aspect of your life: you couldn't possibly have known the outcome before it even happened. You hoped for the best, actively participated, and the Universe gave it to someone else. It doesn't have anything to do with you. Just buy yourself some flowers on the way home and brush your shoulders off. Tomorrow is a fresh day.

Be Selfish, Not a Martyr

So, the other thing about Tina, Amy, and Bethenny that I LOVE (PRIASE HANDS) is while they all proclaim to live by a "yes to life" code, they aren't afraid to do what is best for themselves. They have all been accused of being that word that people love to call women who are strong and intimidating. And they all have embraced it. And, yes, maybe doing what is best for yourself is selfish. And if that's the case, feel free to add me to the list. Maybe more women should be selfish. What if it was actually better for everyone when we act honestly and with our own best interests in mind, than when we stockpile a list of things we sacrificed for other people just so we can hold it over them.

So, we're back here again: saying yes. Once a bunch of my friends were out and trying to figure out our next move. People were shouting out lots of suggestions. They all sounded good to me. And my friend, Josh, who is one of the most rooted, self-assured people I have ever met, just looked at me and said, "Now you're just saying yes to everything." He did not mean it as a compliment. And he was totally right. Saying yes that much, to lots of things indiscriminately, had become a liability. It was not helpful, and it made my word less trustworthy.

Discernment means you are paying attention. Saying yes to everything is suspicious. Rarely does anyone want to do everything *exactly* the same. There is usually a *hint* of preference. People trust people with informed opinions. Doesn't meant we have to listen to them all the time (or ever), but it shows you're both paying attention and telling the truth. Both of these are *key* to getting out of the dark side. People who say yes to everything cannot be trusted – it means they are not paying attention and/or they are not telling the truth.

One time a coach friend of mine called me because she was all torn up about something. She was trying to help out a new coach who was just getting started. The new coach seemed really excited to have help and someone taking interest in her, so she would email my friend with all kinds of requests. What did she think of this? How had she gotten her first speaking gig? Would she proofread her web copy? Granted, the things she was asking got a little cray, but my friend – *wanting to be nice and friendly and life coach-like* – never said no. Now she was all annoyed because she was constantly being asked to do things she didn't want to do. She desperately wanted to say no, but she was also afraid of being disliked by the new girl. Her politely raised, Midwestern self wanted to be nice and helpful and accommodating.

No wonder she called her New York friend for help.

Being nice does not always mean you are acting from a place of integrity. Being nice does not always mean you are being honest. Being nice does not always mean you will be liked. If you just want people to like you, you will end up sacrificing yourself. If you want to like yourself, you might have to sacrifice other people. I believe that the choice between being honest and being nice is not a choice. The dark side is so much more inclined to take care of other people before we take care of ourselves, because it still thinks we don't deserve what we want. But we do.

Ironically, if you want people to like you, start being more honest. As stupid as people can be, they are not dumb. Most of the time they can tell when someone is lying, even when it's not a big deal. Don't be that person who lies for no reason. There's just no need. Keep telling the truth. Everyone else will be fine.

Another example of how martyrdom can show up is through being accommodating. How innocuous does that sound? I have a friend who prides herself on being accommodating. She is always the first to offer help, volunteer to get mail while someone is on vacation, help someone move, etc. She is also usually the first to cancel. Because it's impossible to actually be that accommodating. But she wants to be known as the one you can count on. She spends tons of time saying she is there for other people and almost zero time actually *being* there for them. I would rather someone trust me and think I could use more tact than think I'm Mother Teresa but always wonder whether or not I'll show up.

So, say yes to hard choices. Say yes to the belief that something more beautiful and powerful will come along. Say yes to that thing you want to do even though you don't quite understand it and it makes no sense. Say yes to all your mistakes, the ones you made and the ones you're going to make. Say yes to situations that make you feel vain or self-indulgent.

Yes, to all the times I took on other people's energy and ignored my own. Yes, to all the times I sacrificed myself so other people could feel comfortable and get what they needed. No, to things I think will make me look good to others. Yes, to the things that make me proud of myself.

Be Impeccable with Your Word

Actually just read all of *The Four Agreements* by Miguel Ruiz. It's an incredible book, one that's profound in its simplicity as well as simply profound. But being impeccable with your word is a great start. Do not say yes to things you don't want to do. Do not tell people you love them when you don't. Do not apologize when you have nothing to be sorry for. Do not forgive someone when you're not ready to. Don't say you'll do something full well knowing you won't. Say what you mean and mean what you say. Everyone will be fine. And if they're not, they'll get over it. Or simply move on. Maybe even move on from you. But you have to take care of yourself. And telling lies has never been on anyone's list of self-care.

Define Your "Everyone"

Sometimes when we're hesitant about doing something, it's because we already have an idea in our head that certain people will disapprove. Sometimes we know exactly who we're thinking of when we're trying to avoid judgment; sometimes we globalize with a "they" or an "everyone." Next time you find yourself not acting because you think "they will think it's stupid" or "everyone says that never works," take a minute and think about who exactly it is you're referring to.

Similar to the Naming Your Fears exercise at the beginning of the book, this works for the same reason. It takes an unknown fear that might seem larger than life and quantifies it. It's harder to be endlessly afraid of known entities. Also, chances are your "they" consists of people you know, and if they knew they were the specific reason you weren't doing something, they would feel terrible. If there's a specific reason why you're afraid they would judge you, maybe use the exercise from Chapter 3 and see what's behind that thought. Maybe it's something that isn't serving you anymore and you can work on letting go of it.

Turtle Steps, Celebrate Progress

One thing I have learned is how long it takes me to do things. I have also learned that I am no hero. I am not going to have an epic to-do list that I live and die by. In fact, I don't even have a regular to-do list, because lists stress me out and if something is really important, I'll remember to do it. (Or I won't, and am probably forgetting a lot of things. But, if I'm forgetting them, were they really that important to begin with? Maybe most things just aren't that big of a deal.)

Martha Beck also calls these "Turtle Steps" – breaking something down into small enough, manageable enough chunks that you can do each one pretty effortlessly, or at least with minimal stress. The idea is that lots and lots of tiny, practically unnoticeable steps add up to big actions. Actions that are way too overwhelming to consider doing at the onset can be broken down into steps that actually have a chance of happening. I don't know about you, but this is the kind of process works for my brain. It makes my life disciplined, but also very easy.

You might get more stuff done in a day than I do. I am very okay with this. But if you are a person who struggles to get things done and feel accomplished, think about all the things you might need to do to get something done and then sit down with your calendar. Make your commitments small enough that keeping them won't be too much on a problem. Always err on the side of ease. I already know I will never be able to sit and write for eight hours. Or four hours. Or even two hours. So I don't try and pretend I will turn into that person. Or make myself feel bad for being that person. I write for one to two hours, then I send some emails, and have a few client sessions. That's an awesome day for me.

What's an awesome day for you? How can you break down the things you want to do into small enough tasks so they have a tinge of manageability, while also a likelihood of getting done? And, for the love of God, don't forget to give yourself a treat every time you finish something. Everyone loves treats. So do you.

Almost all of my clients scoff at the Turtle Steps when I introduce them. We break something they want to do or to achieve into very small steps over a moderate period of time, and almost without fail, they say, "I could do that tomorrow. How about I just do that tomorrow, and then we'll come up with a couple more things I can do?" Because. Maybe that's the reason the thing is still hanging over their heads. Maybe it will take a few more days than you would ideally like it to, but maybe it also means that this time it will actually get done. Sometimes we test drive using their way and then using turtle steps. I don't think I need to tell you which one usually works.

100 Rejections Project

Last October, I was very fortunate to be at a dinner event with a lot of brilliant ladies. The event was hosted by a well-known life coach who was also one of my teachers during my Life Coach Training. She is not based in New York and rarely comes to town, so I jumped at the opportunity to get in some face time.

It was a beautiful event, held in a beautiful apartment with beautiful views and lots of beautiful, intelligent women. One woman in particular stood out because (as it was told to me) she had an inspiring story about building her business. She was aware that her fear of putting herself out there was hindering her success, so she created a challenge for herself. She called it "100 Rejections." Since she was so afraid of being rejected, her goal became to hear the word "no" as much as possible. So she began mindfully putting herself out there. She took risks, she ventured out of her comfort zone – all with the specific intention of being told "no."

I mean...how amazing is that?

The thing is, she never got to 100 Rejections. Because the more she put herself out there, the more comfortable she became with herself, the less people rejected her and the more they wanted to collaborate with her. The more she welcomed rejection, the more it eluded her. She took the thing she was afraid of the most, and made it the goal.

You guys. This might actually be the key to everything.

Something to Try: Pick One Thing, Get Specific

Identify one thing you want. Could be a big-ish thing, but get very specific. Can you break it down into at least five very small steps that seem super-manageable compared to thinking about the thing you want? The goal is to take steps so small you barely have to think about them – and then they're done. The more specific, the better. Do the first one of those steps tomorrow. Schedule the remaining four things throughout your week. Don't do more than one per day.

For more exercises, recordings, and pretty worksheets, hop over to sarakravitz.com/toolkit and download the toolkit now!

Chapter 7

No One Cares

"The great epochs in our lives are at the points when we gain the courage to rebaptize our badness as the best in us."
– Friedrich Nietzsche

I ronically enough, the same person who is credited for "follow your bliss" is also the same one who wrote: "It is by going down into the abyss that you recover the treasures of life. Where you stumble, there lies your treasure." Not many people ever really talk about that part, and yet Joseph Campbell (same guy) is one of the ones that does. Imagine the abyss is your dark side. The parts of yourself you keep hidden or tucked away because you think something is wrong with them. Of course, those wind up being the very things you need to get to what's next for you. That's just the kind of world we live in. How amazing is that?

Be Proud Because You Did It

Basically, this whole book can be boiled down to a Nike slogan: Just do it. Just do the thing you think everyone will laugh at. Or makes no sense. Or you're too old to do. I hope it's hard enough that you get something out of it. I hope your dark side rises up around you and teaches you everything you need to know. Because the truth is, the thing you're afraid to do, the thing you think will make other people not like you or you not like yourself, is the path forward.

If the darkness of a moment is too much, look to the outcome. Look to how the outcome will make you feel. Work toward that. You might have the tools to question your thoughts or self-coach. You might genuinely know better, but even so, sometimes a moment can knock you down and it's hard to find your footing. In those moments, look to the outcome.

No, the outcome might not happen the way you think it will, but the feeling you're trying to bring into your life isn't wrong. Remember in *The Matrix,* when the Oracle told Neo only what he needed to hear? She didn't tell him he was The One (should there have been a spoiler alert? It's almost been ten years. Can I assume we all know what happens in *The Matrix* by now?). She knew it wouldn't be helpful to him. She told him the thing that was. So maybe that's what Mindy was for me. I was never going to be an Ob-Gyn. You will probably not be The One. But sometimes the things we need to hear to get us on the right path are not what we thought they would be.

The Dark Side Is Your Ticket to Freedom

It's where all the good stuff is. Growth is interesting, plateauing is boring. Energy needs to shift and move; stagnancy is where we begin to suffocate. We are here to be challenged and satisfied. To feel like we're accomplishing things. We're not afraid of work, we're worn out by busy work. We're tired of working relentlessly on the wrong things. We don't need work to be easy. We want to feel like we are helping, or doing something worthwhile, instead of just spinning our wheels and waiting for something to change. Work gets so much of our time and energy; of course we'd rather it be something we enjoy.

Here is where we also talk about the unknown: the things that haven't happened yet that we can have no way of knowing what they might look like or how they might show up. And this is where you might imagine yourself feeling around in the dark, with only the feelings in your body to guide you. Imagine you could feel your way through the dark. Not with your arms outstretched in front of you, bumping into physical objects, but with feelings in your body, your gut, your instincts.

If you stood still enough, long enough, would your body show you the way? Not with your eyes or your brain, but with your feelings. Like, this feels like a good way to go. Let's go there. This feels like a bad way to go, let's avoid this. The path that feels good is paved with warm, free, light feelings. The path away from where you want to go is also lined with feelings, but these feel more restrictive, colder, more repulsive. Both have a lot to teach you, but which one do you want to follow? This is not a leading question. You might want to follow the "bad" path for a while, just to see what would happen. And that is fine.

This is why the tools and exercises in this book are so key. You've probably been using one set of faculties to make decisions about what to do and what to think about what you've done. Here, we can introduce a whole new way to collect data and implement changes. Naming Your Fears helps you figure out what exactly it is you're dealing with, so you can begin to dismantle it. Identifying exactly what it is can make it less powerful and maybe something you can begin to work with. The Body Compass can help you understand things that you may have been only able to get so far with using your brain alone. The Work can help you process thoughts or judgments about past, present, or future circumstances, and help you see them in a new light that will ultimately just be more helpful for you. Turtle Steps are so important. It can be a whole new way to get things done. The thing you want might not exist yet, so of course you won't know what to look for. But that doesn't mean you can't still head in the direction of what it feels like. Telling the truth and taking small steps toward the positive feelings in your body are key for navigating the unknown.

So, Let's Review

Here are the tools you've learned and exercises we've covered:

First, Name Your Fears – the thoughts/things you're trying to avoid the most. Bring into focus what exactly that you're dealing with. You might never fully banish a fear, but if you know its name, what it looks like, and how it behaves, you'll probably take it less seriously.

Second, calibrate your Body Compass. If your brain is slightly occupied with panic, let's bring in your body as a guide toward things you might want to consider for next steps, and away from those that might be less helpful.

Third, let's start to question some of the thoughts your brain is supplying you with that might be keeping you stuck. Are they painful? Are they helpful? Are there alternatives that might be just as true and, coincidentally, happen to be a lot more helpful?

Four, move. Move your body. Quiet your brain. It might be strange, but lean into it. Give something else a chance to run the show for a bit. You never know what might come through.

Fifth, find three beautiful items, activities, or experiences and bring them into your day-to-day experience. Infuse your life with a little beauty and luxury. It's not only okay, it's essential. Allow it to help elevate everything else.

Sixth, identify one thing you might want to pursue. Could be anything, but make sure it's something you actually want and not something you think you should want. Break it down into lots of teeny, tiny steps. Do one step a day. Or every other day. Whatever feels the easiest to you. Relish the knowledge that you are making progress and moving forward toward something you want.

Repeat as necessary.

Some Parting Sentiments

Sunlight Is a Natural Antiseptic

In her book, *Carry On, Warrior: Thoughts on Life Unarmed*, Glennon Doyle Melton uses the sunrise to talk about the unwavering presence of God's love. Whether or not you believe in God, it's beautiful way to imagine the grace we can take part in every day. She writes:

> *"That sun shows up every morning, no matter how bad you've been the night before. It shines without judgment. It never withholds…. You can hide from the sun, but it won't take it personally. It'll never, ever punish you for hiding. You can stay in the dark for years or decades, and when you finally step outside, it'll be there. It was there the whole time, shining and shining. It'll still be there, steady and bright as ever, just waiting for you to notice, to come out, to be warmed."*

HOW BEAUTIFUL IS THAT?!? The light is not conditional. It was there, it will be there. It will come and burn off the fog, dry up the rain, bleach away the mold and the mildew. I often stand on street corners, waiting for the light to change, and turn my face to the sun, almost as a prayer. The night will come, and so will the sun. Take what you will from both, but don't believe the darkness is any truer than the light.

Be Scared, Say Yes Anyway

When to say yes: when things feel scary and there's an overpowering urge inside you saying "yes" and either you don't know why or you know exactly why. When somehow you can sense that going against it will crush your soul in a way that you're not totally prepared to do. Or you know that for some reason the damages will be too much and you will have separated from yourself in a way that will take a long time to recover from.

To feel that powerful "yes" and ignore it anyway is dark. To divorce from yourself at that level is to abandon yourself in a way that you might not want to get used to. Even though your brain might be comfortable in patterns of safety, with keeping yourself small, or with making you pay for all the terrible decisions that have led to this moment, say yes.

What would you like to be associated with? What makes you feel more like you? What will keep you interested enough to grow and be terrible at and have to start over and you'd still do it? What will humble you? What will make you really proud when you've worked super hard and it's over? And then the second it's over, you're thinking about the next thing. Because, if we're lucky, this is a cycle that continues over and over again.

Design or Default

If we are lucky, life will happen. It will be long and eventful and hopefully, relatively, pain-free. During this time, why don't you pick out a few things you'd like to do along the way? Doesn't have to be nothing, doesn't have to be everything, but why not make it something? We'll be here for a bit, so why don't you plan for some of the time you're here? If they don't work, they don't work. If they do and they're awesome, pick some new ones. Life will happen anyway, so play a role in yours.

Every Moment Is a Moment to Begin Again

One of my favorite yoga teachers used to say that: "Every moment is a moment to begin again." The last moment is gone.

It's over and it's not coming back. For better or worse, it's now in the past. Nothing can be done, or changed, or fixed. So focus on the present moment. On these actual words that you're reading. This very word. This word right now is your present moment. Every single thing you've ever done cannot be changed, so stop trying to change it. It's literally impossible. Make your amends, say thank you, and then let time do its work. Focus on your present. It's the only thing you can do anything about. Set yourself free. Let yourself off the hook. Onward.

Ignore Everyone

Free your soul. That's the only game around. Get free. Just continue to get free. All day, every day. There will always be eyes on you. You cannot let it compromise you. No one actually cares what you do. They're just using you to justify their own choices – to see where they fit and measure up. If you start growing, they might feel like they have to grow. And growth can be scary, so they'll shame you into keeping you where you are. They might not even mean to, but it's a self-preservation technique. They sense that the life they know is dying, so they're trying to save themselves. Disregard them. Let them watch. Do not listen. Get free anyway.

I Believe You Are Brave Enough

Girl, you can do hard things. I know you can. The bravest thing you can do is be who you are – cheesy, stupid desires and all. We need you. I need you. I cannot be brave without you being brave. You might be someone very different than you thought you were, and that's okay. It's better than okay.

Mostly because it means you've stopped forcing yourself into a mold you think you should fit in. I expected myself to "figure things out" a long time okay. Guess what? I never did. Because "figuring it out" never looked like my life does now. But my life is beautiful and valid. What was in my way was the expectation that it would look like something else.

I hope you do something for no other reason than because you want to. That you read this book and go a little easier on yourself. That you accept you have gifts no one else has. Or, even if they do, you understand that we need lots of different kinds of these gifts. I hope you start to live by a metric of ease vs. a metric of busy.

Because maybe it's not about knowing more. Maybe it's about knowing less. As adults, we cling to any tiny thing we may have learned along the way, or found true at one point. We hold fast to those nuggets, as part of a larger hope that we will never again find ourselves in the dark. We hold on to a tiny glimmer of light, and even as it gets dimmer, we refuse to let go. If we knew that letting go would bring a whole new dawn, of course we would let go. But when we are scared of the dark, we will huddle around a dying match. Maybe somewhere deep down we know it's not sustainable, but it's there, so at least for that second we don't have to worry about it.

Remember, fear leads to bravery. Say yes and figure it out later. The dark side is where all the good stuff is. It's not too late for you to find out what you want and to actually be able to do something about it. This is good, necessary work. You deserve to have a life that makes you proud of who you are and what you've done. This book will get you there. I promise.

Further Reading

Finding Your Own North Star: Claiming the Life You Were Meant to Live by Martha Beck

Steering by Starlight: The Science and Magic of Finding Your Destiny by Martha Beck

Carry On, Warrior by Glennon Doyle Melton

Loving What Is by Byron Katie

The Four Agreements by Don Ruiz

The Artist's Way by Julia Cameron

Daring Greatly by Brené Brown

Big Magic by Elizabeth Gilbert

The Most of Nora Ephron by Nora Ephron

The Life-Changing Magic of Tidying Up: The Japanese Art of Decluttering and Organizing by Marie Kondo

Tiny Beautiful Things: Advice on Love and Life from Dear Sugar by Cheryl Strayed

Bossypants by Tina Fey

Yes Please by Amy Poehler

Pronoia Is the Antidote for Paranoia, Revised and Expanded: How the Whole World Is Conspiring to Shower You with Blessings by Rob Brezny

Create Your Own Luck by Susan Hyatt

A New Earth: Awakening to Your Life's Purpose by Eckhart Tolle

Acknowledgments

First, I would like to thank Angela Lauria for creating this process and for giving me the opportunity to write a book, share it with the world, and hopefully make a difference for someone somewhere. You are brave and wise and strong.

To Maggie, for being patient, sensitive, and kind throughout this process. Thank you for taking a lot of words and helping turn them into a book. Your support and feedback were crucial, and I am deeply appreciative of them.

To my friends, who love me even though, and because, I'm crazy. The Plincies, Skull Life, Bates crew, and Housewives crew – You all are funniest, most supportive people around. I am blessed beyond blessed.

And a million thank yous to all the authors on the Recommended Reading list. Please read all of their books (and watch their shows!). Without their brilliance, wisdom, and insight that has taught me so much, this book wouldn't exist. Or it would just be really terrible.

And to my parents, who deserve to be in every section where it's possible to acknowledge and thank someone. Because it's literally not possible to thank them enough.

To the Morgan James Publishing team: Special thanks to David Hancock, CEO & Founder for believing in me and my message. To my Managing Editor, Gayle West, thanks for making the process seamless and easy. Many more thanks to everyone else, but especially Jim Howard, Bethany Marshall, and Nickcole Watkins.

About the Author

A certified life coach, Sara helps her clients embrace all the things they think they need to change before they can figure out what they really want. She believes humor, realness, and *Friday Night Lights* quotes are the best way to do this.

After spending years working at jobs she mostly liked but never wanted to stay in, Sara finally accepted that all she wanted to do was write books and help people feel empowered. She now helps other people figure out and accept what they really want to and bring more of that into their lives. Yes, we all want world peace, but we also want lattes. These things do not have to be mutually exclusive.

Website: www.sarakravitz.com/
Book: http://www.justtellmewhatiwant.com/
Email: sara@justtellmewhatiwant.com

Thank You

Throughout this book, you probably noticed suggestions to download my toolkit in order to complete an exercise that might help you better understand some of the concepts presented in the chapters. I hope you download the toolkit and give these a shot!

What's also in the toolkit are audio and video tools with other tips and tricks to try that sometimes a book just doesn't have space for. You'll get extra ideas, challenges, explanations – all in one place. These will also help you get a better understanding of what you want, and how to get it. Plus, different exercises can resonate at different times, so you might want to try them a few times.

Working with me is just like this book, only you get results even faster thanks to more personalized attention and a laser sharp focus. If you've read the book, but are having trouble holding yourself accountable through the exercises, you might prefer to work with a real live person to help guide you through the process. Or, if you read the book and are wondering if we should be working together, take the quiz below:

1. Do you feel like you're working just to pay bills?

2. Do you feel like there's more you could be doing with your life?
3. Do you have wants that you're afraid to tell people?
4. Do you feel like it's too late for you to figure out what you want and to actually be able to do something about it?
5. Do you want things to be different but still aren't really sure how to go about doing that?

If you answered "yes" to more than one of these questions, let's chat. This is not what your life is meant to look like, so let's figure out the how we can get you from where you are to where you're supposed to be.

I'd love to hear more about you and your situation, so send me an email at sk@sarakravitz.com and we'll set up a time to talk.

Morgan James
Speakers Group

We connect Morgan James published
authors with live and online events
and audiences whom will benefit
from their expertise.

9 781683 504900